Responses to 101 Questions on Hinduism

John Renard

PAULIST PRESS
New York/Mahwah, N.J.

Cover designs for this series are
by James Brisson Design & Production, Williamsville, Vermont

Library of Congress Cataloging-in-Publication Data

Renard, John, 1944–
   Responses to 101 questions on Hinduism / by John Renard.
     p. cm.
   Includes bibliographical references and index.
   ISBN 0–8091–3845–X (alk. paper)
    1. Hinduism. I. Title.
BL1210.R44   1999
294.5—dc21
                                      98–49026
                                         CIP

Published by Paulist Press
997 Macarthur Boulevard
Mahwah, New Jersey 07430

www.paulistpress.com

Printed and bound in the
United States of America

CONTENTS

iii

Dedicated to the Memory of
Richard F. Smith, S.J. (1920–97)
Louis A. Barth, S.J. (1919–96)
and
Francis J. Corley, S.J. (1909–72)
who invited their students at
Saint Louis University
to a wider world of thought and belief

PREFACE

As part of a matched set, this volume arranges questions in nine sections to parallel the structures of its companion volumes on Islam and Buddhism. The first two sections give ilitui il al background about the beginnings and spread of Hinduism, along with a discussion of the Hindu scriptures. Sections three through five deal with a host of matters relating to doctrine, ritual, legal and ethical problems, and spirituality. Part six explores the ways in which the Hindu tradition has contributed to the various fields of humanistic learning and the arts. Section seven discusses Hinduism's manifold relationships with various other traditions, beginning with those that developed in the Hindu milieu (Buddhism, Jainism, Sikhism), and others that came into contact with Hinduism from outside India (Christianity and Islam). A section is dedicated to matters especially pertinent to women and the family. Finally, various items of more recent interest fill part nine. In the interest of simplicity I have opted for a type of minimalist transliteration intended to help toward something at least approaching correct pronunciation. I have attempted to keep italics to a minimum, italicizing technical terms on first appearance and otherwise only when making a technical point. Unless designated B.C.E., all dates are C.E.

My thanks first of all to those unnamed specialists in Hinduism, some of whose books are listed in suggestions for further reading, on whose work I have relied so heavily. I am grateful in a more personal way to a number of people: John Borelli (whom I thank especially for his generous reading and helpful suggestions), Gerry Carney, David Carpenter, William Cenkner, Frank Clooney, Fred Clothey, Mariasusai Dhavamony, Diana Eck, Jim Redington, and Dan Sheridan—who

1

through their lectures, publications, and collegial discussion have made the study of Hinduism so intriguing and accessible.

To the College of Arts and Sciences of Saint Louis University I am grateful for the time and resources made available by the Eugene Hotfelder Professorship in the Humanities. Special thanks go to David Vila of Saint Louis University for the superb editorial skills with which he expedited the completion of this project, for his compilation of the index, and for providing the various summary charts. Thanks also to Mindi Grieser of Saint Louis University for proofreading the text. And as always, thanks beyond words to my wife, Mary Pat, for her good humor, encouragement, and companionship.

ONE:

BEGINNINGS AND EARLY SOURCES

THE 101 QUESTIONS AND RESPONSES

1. Why should I try to learn about something so strange and far away as Hinduism? And how did you get interested in it?

Nearly a sixth of the world's population identify themselves in some way with the various faith traditions that now comprise "Hinduism." That alone would recommend its study to anyone interested in the religious aspects of the story of humankind. But Hinduism is important for several other large reasons as well. Out of it have grown a number of other religious traditions whose adherents think of themselves explicitly as not-Hindu, namely, Buddhism, Jainism, and Sikhism. Though the latter two have not grown significantly outside the Indian subcontinent, Buddhism carried aspects of Hinduism's theo-mythic legacy with it on its missionary odyssey throughout East and Southeast Asia. One could argue persuasively that a serious appreciation of Buddhism requires at least a general familiarity with the *dramatis personae* of Hindu theology. Even apart from its far-reaching impact on Buddhism, Hinduism's immense richness and mythic vitality have the potential to open still further the mind of any willing student of religion.

Ever since the Beatles discovered the Maharishi, one thing has been increasingly clear about Hinduism: it isn't just in India any more. In recent times, various mission-oriented movements within Hinduism, together with an ever more mobile world population, have contributed to its slow but steady growth in Europe and the Americas. But, you ask, how do I begin to make sense of this reality that still seems as culturally foreign as it once was geographically distant? By listening to the story of a segment of the human race too large and too interesting to ignore. And by keeping in mind from the start that whatever your immediate impressions of this vast and colorful tradition, Hinduism is always more than what it appears to be.

Hinduism is the term commonly used to designate a wide variety of religious phenomena of Indian origin dating back over three thousand years. So diverse are these phenomena that some scholars prefer to speak of "Hinduisms," but I will use the term "greater Hinduism." My interest in this tradition dates back to a university course in 1967 that included a large segment devoted to surveying major non-Christian religious traditions. The following year I began my teaching career at a Jesuit high school and was assigned to teach a unit on "world religions." Through these thirty years I have remained intrigued with Hinduism, teaching various aspects of it in survey courses on religious traditions of Asia and on religious art at the secondary, college, and adult education levels and as a component in several graduate courses in non-Christian spirituality and comparative theology. During the early 1970s I had decided on a career in religious studies, but was searching for a way to decide among Hinduism, Buddhism, and Islam. My path led me to focus on Islamic studies because of the enormous size, global importance, and rate of growth of Islam. But Islam's intimate connections with Hinduism during several periods of Indian history, and the growing importance of establishing as broad a context as possible for theological education have kept me coming back to Hinduism. Over the years I have enjoyed opportunities to travel in south and southeast Asia, to take courses on Hinduism, and to discover that Sanskrit was much too complex a language to learn on my own. The experience of dipping into this amazing religious and cultural tradition both professionally and as a kind of hobby has been enormously rewarding. I hope these pages will offer a glimpse of the "greater Hinduism" that has adorned this earth for so long and is surely here to stay.

2. Where and when did Hinduism begin? Did it have a "founder," like Jesus or Muhammad or Buddha?

If faith traditions were books, Christianity would be a large anthology, Hinduism an encyclopedia. Vast and variegated as the phenomenon of Christianity is, the forms of religious belief and practice typically identified as Hinduism run an extraordinary gamut. And the lack of unity that Christians often find tragic or scandalous in their heritage, Hindus as often relish in theirs. What matters most for Hindus is not what people believe and how they express it, but *that* they believe in an order greater than the human mind can fathom or spirit can dominate. The name "Hindu" derives etymologically from a root that means "to flow," as a river does. It referred to the Indo-Pakistani region called "Sindh" and the great stream called the "Indus" that flows through it. Hinduism has simply become a convenient, and relatively recent, way of referring to the complex tradition of faith communities that developed in the earliest centers of civilization throughout the Indian subcontinent.

It is virtually impossible to date the origins of Hinduism. We naturally tend to identify the origins of Buddhism, Christianity, and Islam with the lifetimes of their founding figures. But since the record of history attributes to no individual or group anything like a foundational impulse or teaching, the best one can do is fall back on "circumstantial" evidence from archaeology and broad changes in the social and cultural landscape. Traces of early urban Indus valley settlements suggest polytheistic beliefs that included pastoral gods and fertility goddesses. Throughout the Indian subcontinent, peoples of perhaps Central Asian origin called Dravidians cultivated the favor of regional "chthonic" ("earthy") deities presiding over farm and pasture, mountain and sea, and placated the prickly spirits inhabiting rivers and trees and other more localized realms of nature.

Archaeological and other evidence from perhaps as far back as the third millennium B.C.E. points to an early Aryan culture in the north and northwest regions of the Indian subcontinent, whose language and pantheon bore important similarities to those of classical Greece and Rome. Their deities personified forces of nature, arranged in a hierarchy dominated by the lords of the upper regions. Society was likewise stratified into what would eventually become India's caste system. Over the space of several centuries, Aryan myth and religion developed into the basis of the Brahmanical tradition. Moving south slowly and peacefully, Aryan culture blended with Dravidian and other cultures, gradually dispersing institutional features such as social stratification. This is, in very rough outline, the earliest entry in the encyclopedia of religion that we now call Hinduism.

3. Did the early Hindus have sacred texts? How did they develop and what was their purpose?

The earliest literature in Sanskrit, the Indo-European language of the Aryans, is a collection of texts called "Veda," a word related to our "wisdom" and "vision" via the Latin *videre,* "to see." In the very distant past, quasi-mythic figures called the *rishis* (sages or seers) composed the first texts that eventually came to constitute four collections *(samhita)* known as Vedas. The sacred authors were believed to be inspired in the sense that they "heard" the sounds of the Sanskrit hymns communicating an eternal message that pervaded the cosmos. Here begins the larger classification of Hindu scripture called *shruti,* that which is heard and recited—that is, experienced directly. Even though the tradition acknowledges human involvement in the composition of the Vedas, Hindus consider the sacred texts inerrant because they are not of human origin.

An anthology of just over a thousand hymns *(rig)* arranged in ten books (literally, *mandalas*) called the *Rig Veda* was the first to be compiled. These hymns formed the basic text of rituals led by hereditary priests called Hotri ("pourers" of the libation), whose task was to call on the sacred powers by recitation. Over the next two centuries or so, three other Vedic collections developed, apparently in response to the gradual division of ritual tasks among several types of officiants.

First, since sound was so critical in liturgical practice, a group of sound specialists called Udgatri priests developed. The *Sama Veda,* second of the four scriptures, consists mostly of hymns taken from the *Rig Veda* and arranged according to the "melodies" *(samans)* and poetic meters essential to ritual efficacy. As ritual specialization proceeded, a class of priests called the Adhvaryu took over various ritual actions that they performed while uttering sacred formulae, or mantras, comprising the third Veda, called the *Yajur.* Finally, Brahmin priests secured and maintained efficacious contact with the spiritual powers called generically *brahman,* by means of the incantations eventually collected in the *Atharva Veda.*

In the full-fledged Vedic sacrificial ritual, each of the four classes of priests would arrange themselves at the four cardinal points around the altar—Hotri on the east, Udgatri on the west, Adhvaryu on the south, and Brahmin on the north—and recite from their designated portion of the scripture.

As in many other traditions, comprehensive "theological" explanations developed as to how these scriptures came to be as they are. Hindus consider the primal scriptures eternal, and as such, they existed in a sort of archetypal form in the mind of God. They were much fuller in their original form, and over the ages suffered regrettable but natural attrition from faulty human memory as well as from the ill intentions of people who could not abide by the revealed message. Legend says that the sage Vyasa rescued the scriptures from perdition by entrusting each Veda to one of his chief pupils.

4. Does the elaborate division of labor in early Hindu ritual reflect a similarly complex social structure in society at large?

"On earth as it is in heaven" might be a handy to way to characterize the parallels the history of religion often reveals between earthly societies and the sacred hierarchies manifest in myth and ritual. Perhaps the earliest reference to social differentiation occurs in the *Rig Veda*. Hymn 10:90 describes the sacrifice of the Primal Person, whose body symbolizes the raw material of all creation. As the cosmic body is dismembered ritually, each part gives rise to some element or power in nature or human occupation. The mouth became the priest (Brahmin) and fire, the arm the soldier, the thigh the farmer, and the soles of the feet the laborer class (Shudra) and earth. Still far from a developed notion of caste as such, this is nonetheless an early indication of a belief in the seamless correspondence among all levels of reality.

The later concept of *varnashramadharma,* the cosmic law *(dharma)* of class *(varna,* literally "color") and station *(ashrama)* would link the four broad types of occupation with that of the four stages in life (student, householder, forest dweller, renunciant), though the latter stages do not apply to all classes equally. When the five or more Aryan tribes moved into India, they brought with them a fairly stratified social structure with priests at the top, but special prominence given to the warrior, and farmers and artisans at the bottom. Addition of the laborer class, the Shudras, apparently provided a way of incorporating the subjugated peoples into the Aryan system. Eventually the Brahmin priestly class came to dominate, and their preeminence remained largely uncontested until at least the sixth century B.C.E. The Brahmins protected their hegemony with elaborate concerns for ceremonial and social purity, going to great lengths in dietary matters and avoiding marriage to non-Brahmins. Brahmin class purity eventually became the basis for the development perhaps between 600 and 300 B.C.E. of the caste system properly so-called.

5. To be so focused on ritual, the people of Vedic times must have felt very much at the mercy of the divine powers. What were those deities like?

Concern with ritual was so precise, at times perhaps even obsessive, as to cross over into the realm of magic. It was truly a matter of life and death. Powers far above human capability pervaded every nook and cranny of daily experience. Survival in the face of the whims and caprices of unapproachable forces seemed to call for extreme care and control in attempts to communicate with the deities. The earliest formal description of a pantheon numbers the principal deities at thirty-three, eleven assigned to each of the three cosmic realms, the sky, the lower atmosphere, and the earth. One systematic breakdown suggests that the thirty-three have Dyaus (as in Zeus) ruling the sky and Prithivi the earth. Eight daughters of the river Ganga (Ganges); eleven Rudras ("terrible ones"), both male and female, who came to represent the fearful aspect of divine power; and twelve celestial (and zodiacal) Adityas ("unbounded ones") led by Varuna and including Indra, Vishnu, and Mitra, make up the total.

Hindu mythology is almost infinitely variable in its descriptions and characterizations of divine forces and presences. Over many centuries the tradition evolved an amazing range of metaphors for talking about the ineffable. What is most important to keep in mind for the moment is that the Vedic pantheon represents only the earlier phases of Hinduism's expansive wisdom about how impossible and at the same time absolutely necessary it is for human beings to try to conceive of the divine. As the tradition developed, certain metaphors (called *namarupa,* name-forms in Sanskrit) emerged into prominence, while others receded into theological oblivion. That is not to say that Hindus think deities merely come and go like the rest of us. It is rather an acknowledgment of the incompleteness of human understanding and the temporary validity of even the most profound human insight.

Given that, the Vedic names and forms of God that have risen to prominence over the long history of Hinduism are, for example, the celestial god Vishnu and the atmospheric Rudra, known as Kapalin ("Skull-holder"), an epithet especially associated with Shiva. Other important Vedic names and forms that have retained some limited importance are the celestial Varuna and atmospheric Indra. Varuna was the all-seeing sustainer of cosmic order and the original head of the pantheon. Indra, addressed in more Vedic hymns than any deity save Agni ("fire"), gradually overtook Varuna. As storm power, Indra posed greater threat and thus perhaps commanded greater attention. In later myth, Indra is in turn vanquished by both Vishnu and Shiva. Other important deities not numbered in the "Thirty-three" but still prominent in the Vedas include the terrestrial Agni, atmospheric Vayu ("wind"), and celestial Surya (the orb of the sun, as distinguished from the sun's various powers). For most ritual purposes, Agni, as the object of the fire ritual that many Hindus continue to practice even several times a day, stands out most of all.

6. Could you describe one or two of the principal deities in greater detail? How did people imagine these beings?

Indra is important not only because of his prominence in the Vedic hymns, with over two hundred devoted to his praise, but because of his persistence in later myth, if only as an antagonist bested by newly ascendant deities. Known from inscriptions as far away as Boghazkoi in central Turkey, Indra was among the earliest deities of the Aryan pantheon. In Vedic myth, he outgrows his original association with control of all major atmospheric phenomena to assume the role of invincible warrior and commander of the divine juggernaut. Some scholars link the change to a time when the Aryans were engaged in especially intense campaigns of subjugation of India's indigenous tribes. As global conqueror, Indra is associated with all eight compass points, whereas many early deities are accorded more limited sway; and he becomes the principal lord of the Kshatriya class, the divine counterpart of the Aryan champion.

The reddish or golden-skinned Indra rides, like all the gods, a distinctive "vehicle," either a white horse, an elephant, or a golden chariot. In his four arms he carries the *vajra* (thunderbolt), a lance, and a quiver of arrows with a rainbow as his bow. Legions of stormy godlings called Maruts accompany him as he rides forth to trip up the foolish with the hook and snare of illusion. In his most celebrated and characteristic triumph, Indra quells the serpent demon Vritra, who has held back the cosmic waters, thereby releasing light, dawn, sun, and the sacred intoxicating juice called Soma, along with rain. Indra never became an important subject for sculptors, but appears often in medieval manuscript painting, usually in a subordinate role as one supplanted by Vishnu, Shiva, or Krishna.

A terrestrial deity named Agni (related to the Latin *ignis,* fire) plays a complex role in the mythic theology of the Vedas, appearing in at least two hundred hymns. As fire itself, or the deity whose manifestation is fire, Agni opposes all darkness and evil as he rules the southeast, the point of greatest illumination and heat in the solar course. As both sire and scion of the gods, he is both oldest and youngest, enjoying a second birth each time he is ignited by his ten mothers, who are the kindler's fingers. Ever present in ritual, he is both the benevolent source of the daily Vedic household fire offering and the devouring power of the cremation rite. Since the fire offering involved milk, myths describe Agni as the butter-haired one who eats ghee (clarified butter) with teeth of flame and seven fiery tongues, as he sweeps the earth in a chariot borne aloft on the seven winds. Medieval Hindu sculptors occasionally depicted Agni, usually as a pleasantly smiling but rigidly frontal ascetical-looking figure haloed in the starlike rays of a solar disc. Even though deities such as Indra and Agni represent images of the divine that have largely lost currency, mythic descriptions such as these provide important insights into the imaginative genius of the tradition. An appreciation of how these names and forms of the divine powers change is essential to an understanding of the larger reality called Hinduism.

7. Did any further sacred texts develop out of the Vedas in the way, for example, the Rabbinical literature developed in the process of interpreting the Hebrew scriptures?

The Vedic hymns were only the first of many sacred compositions to appear over more than two millennia. About a dozen large texts called Brahmanas, probably written only after many hymns existed, represent a second phase of scriptural development. Sometimes called the "Hindu Talmud," these prose manuals comment in minutest detail about ancient ritual and helped shore up the position of the priestly class as indispensable practitioners of the sacred arts. They also occasionally develop stories to which Vedic texts allude only in passing. Each Brahmana is attached directly to one of the four Vedas (two to the *Rig,* eight to the *Sama,* two to the *Yajur,* and one to the *Atharva*). One of the *Yajur Veda's* Brahmanas, called the *Shatapatha* ("Hundred Paths") stands out above the rest in religious and theological importance. Finally, a statement from this last Brahmana offers a hint of the status to which the priestly class had been by now elevated: distinguishing between two types of gods, those of heaven and the Brahmins, it goes on to explain that sacrifice is for the heavenly gods and ritual fees for the earthly ones. It is worth noting that the Brahmanas mention Shiva by name for the first time and that Vishnu assumes a somewhat more important role than he had played in the Vedas. These last two deities will eventually become the main divinities in the Hindu pantheon.

A third phase in scriptural development produced the Aranyakas, or "Forest Treatises," so-called because they deal with fairly arcane speculation and refined thinking of the sort best attempted in solitude. A notable feature of these texts is their use of allegorical interpretation of some Vedic texts presented for the individual to meditate on. Attached to, and growing out of, the Brahmanas as the latter are to the Vedas, only four Aranyakas remain. The great significance of these texts for the history of Hinduism is that they represent the beginnings of a reaction to the formalism of Vedic ritual and to the unchallenged rule of the priesthood. This turn was more fully developed in the final phase of the Vedic scriptures, a sizeable body of writings called the Upanishads.

8. Do the earliest Hindu sacred texts contain anything like the Biblical accounts of creation?

While there are a number of Vedic texts that deal with cosmogony, they are very different from the more obvious Biblical parallels. In Genesis, the two creation accounts are prose narratives that proceed with an air of simple factuality, as though the author had been an eye-and-ear witness to the dawn of time and space. The Hindu texts seem more interested in the "why" than the "how" of creation, and they communicate rather a sense of wondering and questioning than of reporting as though on the scene. In addition, the Biblical accounts depict God as directly and physically involved in aspects of the creation. In the Vedic hymns, the world unfolds through a variety of organic metaphors, from the kind of heat generated by a brooding hen, to a golden embryo that splits spontaneously to yield heaven and earth, to the sacrifice of the Primal Person mentioned earlier. Perhaps the most striking is *Rig Veda* hymn 10:129, with its air of mystery and unanswered questions: Who can know these things? If the world came to be even before the gods, what can one say? It ends with the conclusion that no one can know these things and that only the highest gods can do so—and perhaps not even they! The two elements the last text has in common with Genesis are the images of breath as a possible creative power and the existence of a dark watery void in the "beginning." On the other hand, the cosmogonic hymns of the *Rig Veda* are often reminiscent of passages from Job and some of the Prophets, with their tone of wonder and awe.

9. Are there any other similarities between the early Hindu scriptures and the Bible?

Perhaps the single most obvious general parallel in both literary type and religious function is that between the Veda's hymns and the Psalms. In both cases the texts seem intended primarily for liturgical purposes. Both include various genres of poetry. Psalms and Vedic hymns alike praise the divine powers, call out to them for help, lament the apparent triumph of evil and the pervasiveness of suffering, and ask probing questions about the wonders of humanity and the cosmos. In the latter category, a reading of *Atharva Veda* 10:2 in tandem with Psalms like 8 and 139, for example, yields fruitful connections. Both sources also contain elements of mythic narrative, but while mythic themes make up a large portion of the Vedic poems, the Psalms show largely what seem to be residual traces from an earlier time in which the one God of Israel still did battle with a host of rivals (Psalm 29 is very reminiscent of Vedic descriptions of divine dominion over the elements).

Other striking, if less entertaining, parallels appear between ritual texts of the Brahmanas and sections of the Torah especially concerned with rules of purity and proper performance of liturgical ceremony. One could very profitably read Exodus 19–40, the whole of Leviticus, and Numbers 28–36 in connection with Brahmanical descriptions of conditions for efficacious sacrifice and religious etiquette among the priestly class. Reading texts from one tradition in light of similar documents from another invariably underscores significant themes in one's own or kindred tradition, suggesting that what one originally considered alien and incomprehensible is not so odd after all.

10. Can you describe an example of Vedic ritual?

Various forms of sacrifice have always been, and continue to be, an integral part of Hindu religious life. As the Vedic hymn mentioned earlier indicates, religious poets even likened the origins of the cosmos to sacrifice on the grandest scale imaginable. Perhaps the most spectacular, elaborate, and expensive of the great Vedic rituals was the horse sacrifice *(ashvamedha)*. Its purpose could be either the expansion of royal domains or some form of expiation. Preparations began a year in advance. A young white stallion was ritually washed and fed for three days and then set loose to roam, under the watchful eye of the king's retinue. Wherever the horse wandered, there the king would stake his claim, doing battle to secure allegiance if necessary. Assuming success in battle, at the end of the ritual year the horse was brought back to the king's city. At the appearance of the new moon, the king and his principal queen set the actual sacrifice in motion with a midnight vigil. Next day, the horse was decked out and, after a total of 609 other animals of various kinds had been slaughtered, ritually killed. Talk of this sort of extensive carnage strikes most people now as horrific and unthinkable, but bloody sacrifice of a similar nature was once part of the rites of Israel. The role of sacrifice on such a large scale in Hinduism began to change around the sixth century B.C.E., at the end of the Vedic period. World-sustaining offerings would be mostly replaced by sacrifice of a more personal, metaphorical, spiritualized nature, much as the Biblical Prophets reminded Israel that God cared far more about the quality of their relationships than about the aroma of their burnt offerings.

Two:

History and Development

11. You have referred to significant change in Hindu thought that signaled the end of the Vedic period. What sort of change was it and how do we know of it?

During the several centuries from around 800 to 500 B.C.E. further developments in Hindu religious literature give evidence of growing discontent with the spiritual legacy of Vedic ritualism. Earliest hints of this inward turn seem to be the reflections of the Aranyakas, which are more fully developed in the Upanishads. With a Sanskrit compound name that means something like "sitting at the feet of [a teacher]," the Upanishads attached themselves to previous sacred texts, as the Aranyakas and Brahmanas had, in some cases directly to one of the Vedas where no intermediate texts exist. Unlike the Brahmanical texts, however, the Upanishads represented a corrective to, rather than an affirmation of, the Vedic way. Since the Upanishads marked a clear departure from Vedic thinking, it was only much later that they came to be considered the final phase of Vedic literature and thus still revered as *shruti,* "heard" or directly imparted divine wisdom.

Authors of the Upanishads reflect the conviction that the way of ritual action, or *karma-kanda,* espoused by the Vedas and the ancillary Brahmanical literature could not be all there was to religious belief. Some scholars have chosen to refer to the age that produced the Upanishads as an "Axial Period," a time characterized by dramatic advances in thought and awareness of the interiority of the human person, occurring, so it seemed, in various parts of the world. The age of the Upanishads also witnessed the rise of Buddhism and Jainism in India, Confucianism and Taoism in China, Zoroastrianism in Persia, the great Prophets of Israel, and Greek Philosophy, to name the most obvious intellectual and religious advances.

Tradition sets the number of major Upanishads at 108 (a symbolic lunar number associated with the deities), but scholars variously count between ten and thirteen principal works, some prose and some verse. A major theme is the impetus to delve deeper into the nature and causes of existence, the distinctive features of human nature, and the relation of the human to the divine. In search of a unitary explanation to replace the sheer multiplicity of powers that seems to characterize the Vedic worldview, the Upanishads begin to move toward a more unitary worldview. What is the ultimate reality? they asked; what is the self? Is there a faculty within the self that explains what appear to be uniquely human abilities and needs? They began to craft the word *atman* ("breath," later meaning "soul") into a technical term for the indestructible core of the self, and used the word *brahman* to refer to the ultimate reality beyond even the gods themselves. Thus they began to work out a way of understanding the relationship between the individual person and ultimate reality.

Authors of the Upanishads shared with the early Buddhists the view that life in this world was hardly a worthy ultimate goal; there must be a way out of the impasse that was this dead-end suffering. Ritual karma alone would surely get you nowhere, but there must be *some* positive potential to human action. In tandem with the concept, by then well established, of the possibility of endless rebirths *(samsara),* they fashioned the theory that there must be a state beyond waking, dreaming, and even dreamless sleep, in which the self can break free of enslavement to action, in which one experiences simple oneness. Out of their speculation emerged the concept of the intimate relationship between *brahman* and *atman,* to be realized not through karma but through knowledge *(jñana),* achievable through the techniques known collectively as *yoga.* The expression "You are that (reality)" sums up the basic insight. Later tradition came to identify the Upanishads as the culmination or "end of the Vedas" *(vedanta).*

12. What is "Vedanta"? Did it also evolve or did the development of Hinduism end with it?

As a formal school of thought, Vedanta's origins are traditionally attributed to a man named Badarayana, variously dated from the third century B.C.E. to the fifth. Badarayana is credited with underscoring the centrality of knowledge as the only way to liberation. According to his interpretation, the truth taught by the sages is that, through the power of *maya,* brahman creates the phenomenal world of multiplicity, including individual souls, but ignorance prevents human beings from being aware of their true identity and divine origins. It's the question of "the one and the many."

Shankara (d. 820), the interpreter of Vedanta whose views are perhaps the most widely known outside of India, held that *maya,* from a root that means "to measure," causes the mistaken conviction that reality is parceled out into innumerable discrete things and selves who compete for their share of those things. Selves thus accumulate bad karma, which in turn perpetuates the round of rebirths as the only way to make restitution. Maya does not mean that the physical world is somehow all conjured up; the world of one's experience does exist, but as part of a larger reality and not simply as the sheer manyness it appears to be. Suppose that while walking in the forest you become terrified at the sight of a form you are sure is a serpent. You go out of your way to avoid the danger, only to find out later that it was merely a coiled rope. Such is the power of *maya* according to Shankara's interpretation.

In subsequent centuries a number of important thinkers lent distinctive interpretations to the earliest Vedanta. Whereas Shankara seems to have leaned toward a monistic view of the identity of brahman and atman, Ramanuja (d. 1137) allowed for a "qualified" or modified monism; and Madhva (1199–1278) rejected the monism altogether in favor of out-and-out dualistic theism.

13. The Upanishads and Vedanta seem too abstract and arcane to appeal to more than a relatively few people. Surely there must have been more popular developments as well?

Over the course of the millennium and a half that began around 500 B.C.E., Hindu authors produced yet another major group of sacred texts. Of secondary rank, these are called collectively *smriti,* "that which is remembered," representing a form of tradition rather than revelation in the stricter sense. This large category encompasses four theologically and religiously important genres of literature. First are the two major epic poems, the *Mahabharata* ("Great India"), a sort of national saga into which the supremely influential *Bhagavad Gita* ("Song of the Blessed Lord," often referred to as the Fifth Veda) came to be inserted; and the *Ramayana* ("Story of Rama"). Next came the *shastras,* legal and ethical treatises. A group of systematic doctrinal works articulating the views of six philosophical schools in the form of *sutras,* or short pithy statements, appeared during the early and middle centuries of the first millennium. Last came some three dozen works called *Puranas* ("ancient narratives"), eighteen major and eighteen minor with six in each category devoted to one of the three deities who had come to be identified as the *tri-murti* ("triple form"), Brahma, Shiva, and Vishnu. These mythic tales tell of virtually every aspect of the lives of the deities, offering a veritable encyclopedia of Indian culture.

The shastras and sutras served the needs of the specialists in religion, philosophy, and law, but the epics and Puranas had mass appeal and have enjoyed continued popularity through the centuries. Stories of deities and heroic figures entertain by appealing to the imagination and affections, but they also embody a particular kind of theological interpretation that can be expressed fairly simply and directly. That does not mean that the theology behind the popular texts is crass or unsophisticated, merely that it describes a world just close enough to the experience and aspirations of "ordinary" people to engage and captivate them. This is neither the calculating magico-ritual thinking of the Vedic priests nor the detached, rarefied quest for knowledge of monistic Vedanta, but a form of theism populated by a cast of colorful personalities both infinitely attractive and unimaginably fearsome.

On first encountering these stories of the innumerable names and forms of the divine, non-Hindus often react negatively, inclined to dismiss them as mere fables—"myth" in what has unfortunately come to be the worst sense of the word. On the contrary, this is narrative theology at its best, susceptible of immensely subtle and challenging interpretation. Although, for example, the yarns of the mischievous infant Krishna are immediately appealing even to children, they are anything but child's play. As text for the learned and performance for the masses, these stories have borne Hindu religious culture across south and southeast Asia for centuries.

14. With so many stories and divine personalities to choose from, has popular Hinduism developed an equal number of sects or denominations?

Vedic hymns sometimes told stories, so that even from the earliest texts one begins to get a sense of how the "personalities" of the gods vary. All are powerful and successful, but some are naturally more approachable, while others project a dark mystery. All the deities did battle against evil and each had a distinctive largesse in store for the faithful. Over the centuries, however, two deities of very minor importance in the Vedic scheme of things began to emerge from the crowd. Between about 200 B.C.E. and 200 C.E., significant communities developed around devotion to Shiva (the Shaiva) and to Vishnu (the Vaishnava). Shaivite and Vaishnavite communities are only the two largest of many such denominational and sectarian groups within Hinduism.

Shiva, whose name meant "the red one," came to be identified with the characteristics of a particularly formidable Vedic deity called Rudra ("howler," "the terrible") whose name also meant "ruddy" or "reddish." Shaivites see in Shiva unspeakable power and mystery. His dominion over every aspect of life is total, but he is especially associated with the murky depths of death and cosmic entropy, sexuality and rejuvenation. He haunts the cremation ground clad in the loin cloth and ashes of the ascetic, but he is also Nataraja, Lord of the Dance, with a fire that destroys and a drum that regenerates the cosmos continually. Even so, devotees experience great joy in his presence, and I do not want to convey the impression that Shiva, a lunar deity, is the Grim Reaper's twin brother. But compared with the predominant names and forms of Vishnu, those of Shiva tend more toward the awe-inspiring and fearsome. Consequently, as his function in the theological metaphor known as the *tri-murti* (triple-form), Shiva is assigned the role of destroyer, to Brahma's creator and Vishnu's sustainer.

To the Vaishnava community, Vishnu represents the fullness of divinity. Capable of assuming forms of implacable wrath and of destroying any evil force that may arise, this solar deity most often appears as helper and savior. Devotees of Vishnu celebrate his ten most famous, but other countless, *avatara* ("crossing-over-downward") or descents into the realm of human experience in time of direst need. Among non-Hindus, Krishna is probably the most familiar of the avatars, although Vaishnava theology found a way of enfolding Buddhism in its ample embrace by claiming the Buddha as an avatar that Vishnu assumed in order to lead the wicked astray.

Devotees of both Shiva and Vishnu also worship the divine energy *(shakti)*, personified as the various female consorts of their chosen deities. Shiva's feminine aspect takes the names and forms of the lovely Parvati, the redoubtable Durga—slayer of the buffalo demon, and the murderous Kali. Vishnu's principal consort is Lakshmi, who assumes different forms as needed in the stories of Vishnu's various avatars; but he often appears also with Sarasvati, who began her mythic life as wife of Brahma. No significant community ever developed around devotion to Brahma. Often depicted as an old man with four faces, riding a white swan and carrying the Vedas, Brahma remained in the theological background as the revered but disengaged creator.

15. Could you describe Shiva and his devotees in greater detail?

Images of Shiva as Lord of the Dance, embodying in sound and rhythm the life cycle of the cosmos, are probably the most widely known among non-Hindus. Virtually every great museum owns a fetching medieval bronze of the lithe Lord, dancing through a circle of flame, and places it where it will catch the eye of the fortunate visitor who wanders into the Asian collection. Hindus know a world of other names and forms of Shiva that have "acquired taste" written all over them. Shaivite theo-myth is wholly dedicated to helping people conceive the inconceivable, know the unknowable, survive in the presence of the one whose perfect holiness vaporizes the least speck of ungodliness. God is thus totally "other," and yet condescends to dwell in the close confines of the human heart and imagination.

Shiva is the outsider whom even the gods shun, who breaks all categories, as popular theological *via negativa* makes clear. He is no student, for he is married; no householder for he dwells in the cremation ground; no forest dweller, for he drinks to excess; no ascetic, for he carries a weapon; no Shudra, for he wears a snake; no Vaishya, for he is too poor; no Kshatriya, for he destroys rather than protects; no Brahmin, for he does not appear in the Vedas. He is not a woman, for he has a beard; not a eunuch, for he possesses the reproductive power of the linga (phallus); not a youth, for he is ancient and eternal; not old, for he is ageless.

On the other hand, popular stories describe Shiva as both erotic and ascetical, by turns sexually active and abstinent. When his future wife Parvati fails to attract his attention by flirting, she decides to see if self-denial will stir him, sitting in snow during winter, and in fire during summer. At length the two decide to settle into convention and marry, for the two elements of the cosmos must go together. However, Shiva doesn't strike her parents, the Himalayas (Parvati means "mountain daughter"), as right for their daughter. After extended negotiations, they host a procession of other potential suitors, and the gods parade before the mountains. With each dazzling presence, Parvati's mother exclaims mistakenly, "This surely must be Shiva." Finally Shiva appears as an ash-covered ascetic on an aging bull, accompanied by a host of unsavory characters. Parvati's mother faints and then calls it all off, so the gods intervene and persuade Shiva to assume a beautiful form.

Shaivite theology formulated a structural metaphor in which to display all of Shiva's countless apparently contradictory qualities. His first "face" is that of creator, through sexuality and marriage and family. Upholding good against the evil of demonic forces, he displays the face of just wrath. As the power of dissolution in the life cycle of the cosmos, his destructive face reverses creation through asceticism. As master of disguise, the face that obscures and conceals turns vision to forgetfulness. And in the center of the other four faces is that of grace, called the faceless face, symbol of Shiva's utter transcendence.

16. You mentioned that Krishna is one of a number of "avatars" of Vishnu. Could you say more about the cult of Vishnu?

Vishnu—a name said to derive from a root that means either to pervade or to enter into—was a relatively minor Vedic solar deity who was gradually identified with a non-Aryan hero named Vasudeva and a cosmic deity called Narayana. He came to be known especially for his accessibility and willingness to take on virtually whatever form necessary to respond to the needs of his devotees. Millions of Hindus revere Vishnu as himself, so to speak, acknowledging his awe-inspiring yet very approachable power to set all things aright, but his avatars are the focus of many cultic settings. His ten most famous avatars (divine descents into this world) include three in animal form, one in half-human half-animal, and six in human forms. The marvelous stories are vaguely reminiscent of Buddhism's *Jataka* literature, tales of previous lives of the Buddha in each of which he assumes a different salvific form.

The structural metaphor of the avatars has been an umbrella under which Vaishnavite theology has gathered an amazingly wide range of names and forms of the deity as preserved in lore of many origins. Various avatars engage in heroic deeds and battle fiercely to overcome evil, but the most popular of the stories emphasize the deity's irresistible attractiveness, and none more vividly than that of Krishna. In the center-piece of the *Mahabharata* epic, the *Bhagavad Gita,* Krishna appears as the charioteer of Arjuna, a nobleman confronting a terrible moral dilemma: should he fulfill his *dharma* as a warrior even though the enemy are his own kin? Krishna reveals himself as the presence of Vishnu come into the world to confront evil. It is interesting that Krishna makes appearances in the *Mahabharata* prior to and after the *Gita,* but as a mere human prince rather than a deity.

Later popular lore would go on to fill in the details of Krishna's life to provide narrative context and continuity to the episode of the *Gita.* One of the most important of the sacred texts, the ninth or tenth century *Bhagavata Purana,* offers a very complete picture of Krishna's theological significance. His first function is to conquer the demons that beset humankind, usually as the minions of some evil mastermind of an earthling. As he takes on runaway powers of nature, Krishna assumes his place as the first among the gods. But he is also a most forgiving savior, so that even his most hateful enemies are converted into devotees at the merest contact with Krishna.

In illuminating descriptions of the ways in which Krishna can both instill and elicit love, the Purana speaks of a range of appropriate responses to the divine presence: the awe of a worshipper, the feeling of a servant before a master, the love of a parent for a child (or that of a cow for a calf), the love for a dear friend, and even erotic love. But at whatever level one loves Krishna, Krishna's love is infinitely beyond the ordinary. Because he also disappears now and then, Krishna teaches the lover that separation is as exquisite as union, for in distance there is a love born of yearning. In fact, unaware the beloved has merely assumed a different guise, the lover may only imagine the beloved has withdrawn. Besides, Krishna must leave for the good of his devotees, since they cannot bear too much truth at once. The end result of his encounters with his devotees is that Krishna, like Shiva in a way, breaks all the rules and demands that his followers be willing to do the same in order to be with him.

Over the centuries theologians have wrestled with the meaning of the stories, much as specialists in Christology do among Christian the-ologians. Was his coming as Krishna a historical event, or ought one per-haps interpret it all metaphorically?

17. I've heard that there are also many more popular deities important on a more regional or local scale. Who are some of them?

Among the most popular name-forms of the divine is that of the elephant-headed deity called Ganesha. Mythologically speaking he is one of the two sons of Shiva. From a historical perspective Ganesha descended from a class of largely pre-Aryan male spiritual powers associated with strength and fertility. These included heroes *(viras)* as well as their opposite number, enemies of humankind called *rakshasas;* directional guardians called *yakshas;* and a type of minor deity known as *gana* that had its own "lord" *(isha)*, Ganesha. Ganas were originally associated with misfortune and obstruction, but were eventually transformed into the opposite, bringers of luck and removers of obstacles, and Ganesha emerged as a rotund and nonthreatening figure who rides a rat and loves sweets. But whence came the elephant head?

One day Shiva came home and found a handsome young stranger in his house. Not bothering to hear how his wife Parvati had created the youth from the dirt she had scrubbed from her own body, Shiva angrily cut off the young man's head. The gods tell Ganesha to go to the jungle and appropriate the head of the first animal he sees lying down with its head toward the north—and that was an elephant. Another story of the elephant-headed deity says that he gorged himself on sugary rice-balls and went riding on his trusty mount, who then tripped on a snake. Ganesha's stomach popped open so he stuffed the sweets back in and tied himself together with the snake. The moon made fun of Ganesha, so he ripped off one of his tusks and flung it at the orb, shaving off a sliver, so that ever since the moon has not been able to stay full for more than a day or two. Images of Ganesha are very popular, and devotees beseech his aid especially when setting out on journeys or beginning any new venture. In a traditional ritual cluster of five deities called the "five abodes," Ganesha is invoked first even though he is not the chief among them, followed by Vishnu, Shiva, Durga, and Surya (the sun).

Out of that same early class of minor deities from which Ganesha came to prominence, the second son of Shiva, Skanda, also emerged, exhibiting most of all the character of the hero. One story tells how Skanda remained an infant for five days, blossoming on the sixth day into a full-fledged hero to fight a demon. Also known by the name Karttikeya, the celibate warrior and ascetic is often depicted with six heads, armed with bow and arrow, riding into battle on his peacock. But the most important variation on his story calls him Murukan (or Murugan), the name under which he occupies the central position in the most important cult among the Tamil Hindus of southern India. He began his rise to prominence as a deity associated with hunting among people in the southern hills and eventually came to be the preferred name-form of divine power as manifested most of all in his father Shiva. Three very large pilgrimage centers in the south are dedicated to Murukan.

Dozens of other deities, mostly female, are also important, particularly in local settings. Most popular are variations on the theme of divine Mother. Her function, in most of her various forms, is to insure fertility and abundant harvest. In other forms, the Mother can assume fearsome features associated with disease and pestilence (especially smallpox), famine, and death.

18. Has Hinduism ever been directly associated with political structures or regimes?

During the two and a half millennia that began around 700 B.C.E. and ended with the arrival of the British, dozens of Hindu dynasties ruled various parts of India. Kingship's increasingly important role in early mythic literature is in some ways a reflection of the development of political structures. Although there is evidence of kingdoms formed as early as the seventh and sixth centuries B.C.E., the first uncontested political marker is Alexander the Great's invasion in 326 B.C.E. Some early literary evidence suggests the development within Hinduism of the notion of the divinity of kings, a concept that Buddhism and Jainism rejected. It seems clear that the unhappy fates of the Nanda (362–322 B.C.E.), Maurya (322–185 B.C.E.), and Shunga (185–73 B.C.E.) dynasties were intimately tied to intrigues among the priestly retainers at the royal courts, and that under the Mauryan king Ashoka (r. 273–232 B.C.E.) conversion to Buddhism was largely responsible for that tradition's initial spread beyond India. It is almost as clear that the Kushan king Kanishka (r. 120–162) also favored Buddhism. In some dynastic regimes, when succession was not hereditary and in periods of crisis, rulers might be chosen by Brahmans.

The Gupta dynasty and its immediate successor states (320–647), forerunners to the great medieval Hindu Kingdoms, extended their rule over all but the southern third of India. The Chinese

Buddhist monk Fa-Hien, travelling through India in search of ancient Pali texts around the year 400, reports that Buddhism was thriving all over northern India, suggesting broad official tolerance on the part of the Gupta sovereigns, even though they themselves professed devotion to Vishnu. During the fifth century the fortunes of Buddhism in India began to change dramatically, not as a result of active persecution but under the steady influence of the Gupta renaissance of Hindu culture. Invasions by the White Huns during the fifth and sixth centuries gradually weakened the unity of the Gupta empire, and the Huns actively attacked Buddhist institutions. For the next several centuries Buddhism waned, until by 1000 its presence in India was greatly diminished.

After the first Turko-Islamic rulers began to make their presence felt in the late tenth century, Hindu kingdoms began organizing themselves more explicitly along confessional lines, usually in direct response to destruction wrought by Muslim aggressors. A succession of Hindu dynasties ruled central and southern India from the eighth through the thirteenth centuries, maintaining their Hindu identity over against several Muslim sultanates. Muslim rulers made inroads into central and southern India during the fourteenth and fifteenth centuries, and through the sixteenth century the Muslim Mughal dynasty projected its rule over all but the southern third of the peninsula. Important Tamil Hindu states, whose reigns often overlapped, managed to retain control of the far south, including most notably the Pallavas (c. 250–750 as main power, till c. 1250 as petty princes), the Chalukyas (450–1189) and the Cholas (beginnings c. 100, major power c. 800–1300), all of which produced amazing refinements in sculpture and architecture. First to attempt major buildings in stone in the south, the Pallavas built the famous shore temple at Mamallapuram, not far from Madras, and made their capital of Kanchipuram an architectural showpiece. The Chola dynasty is best known for its splendid temple of Shiva in Tanjore and a distinctive style of bronze religious sculpture, whose most famous representatives are flame-circled images of Shiva, Lord of the Dance.

Perhaps the most significant negative result of institutionalized Hindu political power occurred in the form of occasional intra-Hindu sectarian intolerance and periods of persecution of Jains. The most recent association of Hinduism with official government policy appeared during the partition that resulted in the creation of Pakistan as an officially Muslim state in 1947.

19. I've read that Hinduism is part of the religious history of Indonesia and other southeast Asian countries. Does that suggest that Hinduism has had a missionary tradition?

India's spreading cultural and religious influence in what is often called "greater India," especially the regions of southeast Asia now known as Indonesia, Malaysia, and Cambodia, began during the early Christian centuries and proceeded markedly during the Gupta dynasty. Hinduism has never been explicitly missionary-minded the way Christianity, Islam, and even Buddhism have been. And on the whole, the Hindu dynasties were not bent on large scale colonization. The pervasive influence of Indian culture and religion resulted largely from lively trade relations and from the missionary efforts of Buddhist monks. In the new Hinduizing kingdoms, classical Vedic religious practices became popular and local rulers sought to place themselves within royal lineages linking them to Indian blood, even when their actual genealogical connections to India were tenuous at best. In some cases, adventuresome princes of the Hindu warrior caste may have set themselves up as local rulers in their new homes. Shaivite Hinduism seems to have been the predominant branch of the tradition, although major temples appear to have been dedicated to Vishnu, and the reenactment of the largely Vaishnavite themes of the two great epics, *Mahabharata* and *Ramayana,* remains popular still.

An important feature of Hinduism's impact on southeast Asia was its syncretism. In Indonesia and Cambodia, the strong identification of rulers with Shiva especially sometimes even included the worship of the king's personal potency under the symbol of the royal phallus. Hindu kings ruled independently in Sumatra and Java, succumbing only in the fifteenth century to the arrival of Islam. Great temple complexes such as that at Prambanam in central Java remain, along with numerous subtle traces of Hindu influence—in spite of determined attempts by Muslim authorities to purge them from Indonesian society. Around 1300, a Hindu dynasty capitalized on the weakness of the Shailendras, a Buddhist dynasty most famous for its monumental stupa at Barabudur in central Java. By 1365 the kingdom of Majapahit, centered in northeastern Java, had spread to the Malay peninsula and most of the islands of Indonesia. When the Hindu kingdom of Majapahit fell to the Muslims a century and a half later, the king and many Hindu followers fled to Bali, where Hinduism is still practiced.

The kingdom of Champa, covering most of modern Vietnam, survived from c. 150–1471. Still greater Hindu kingdoms began around

100–150 in Cambodia, which eventually ruled Thailand and Laos from about 800 to 1200. Two spectacular temple-cities from the twelfth and thirteenth century in Cambodia proper, Angkor Wat and Angkor Thom, were dedicated to Hindu worship and symbols of the divine kingship of the land's rulers. Hence the name Indo-China. It seems a bit ironic that Buddhism eventually outlasted Hinduism all over southeast Asia after dying out in the land of its birth.

20. Has Hinduism become specially associated with any particular cities, the way Catholicism has with Rome or Islam with Mecca?

Varanasi, more commonly called Banaras, is surely the single most "Hindu" of India's many religiously important cities. Though it is set on the Ganges river, its name is a compound of the names of two local streams, the Varana and Asi. The city is also known as Kashi, after the tribal dynasty whose capital it was. Varanasi's theo-mythic meanings are multilayered. Its founding is especially associated with Shiva, who built it in response to Parvati's request for a home. Many of its fifteen hundred temples are devoted to Shiva himself or deities closely associated with him. Perhaps the most famous of the city's bathing *ghats* on the Ganges takes its name from the "ear-jewel" *(Manikarnika)* Parvati lost there. Like other major religious cities, such as Mecca, Varanasi sits at the center of a larger sacred precinct. Hindu devotees sometimes walk a thirty-six mile perimeter as a symbolic ritual of circumambulation. Pilgrims come to Banaras from all over India to bathe in the sacred Ganges. Countless others wish to be brought there to die, and many Hindu families carry their dead to the bank of the Ganges to cremate them on one of the city's "burning *ghats.*" Varanasi is known also as a gathering place for the religiously learned and their disciples, but since Hinduism has no central teaching authority, the city does not have the "official" magisterial aura of Rome.

As a feature in India's larger sacred geography, Varanasi is one of seven holy cities, each associated with particular deities and important events in their respective myths. Haridvar in the north marks the origins of the Ganges, which is really a deity called Ganga. Ayodhya, near Banaras, the setting for much of the action of the *Ramayana,* is Rama's capital. Mathura, toward the center of India, marks the birthplace of Krishna and a key location in his life story. A ritual circle forty miles in radius, called the Vraj Mandal, with Mathura at its center is the route of

a sixteen-day pilgrimage. To Dvaraka in the far west, Krishna moves as
a young man and becomes the charioteer of the *Gita*. Ujjain, once capital of the Gupta dynasty in the west-midsection of the country, is associated with Shiva and especially with his son Skanda, warrior patron of the
Guptas. Finally, Kanchi on the southeast coast, called the Banaras of the
south, is sacred to Vishnu as well as Shiva. Capital of the Pallava
dynasty, Kanchi houses one of the five most important Shiva lingas. The
role of sacred cities in Hindu tradition is unique in that they map out the
sacred geography of what is now, at least, a single large geopolitical
entity that remains home to the vast majority of the world's Hindus.

21. Has monasticism been a significant factor in the history of Hinduism?

Solitary renunciants have been known in Hindu societies since at
least the later Vedic period, even before the concept of the four life-
stages developed. Toward the end of that idealized career, a man would
withdraw from ordinary involvement for a life of detachment and meditation. The overlapping of the third stage, that of the "forest dweller,"
and the fourth, that of the renunciant or *sannyasi,* suggests a blend of
two traditions. Sannyasis were the early equivalent of solitary monks
called anchorites. During the Upanishadic period, it became common
for small groups of disciples to attach themselves to teachers. Living
together in *ashrams,* they formed the nucleus of what would eventually
become cenobitic orders organized in stable monastic communities.
These communities seem to have influenced the rise of Buddhism and
Jainism, whose early leaders also organized formal monastic institutions
in fixed residences, complete with charters stipulating structures of
authority, dress, and codes of behavior. Wandering "monks" also continued to be associated with all three traditions.

Around 200 a guru named Lakulisha is said to have written an
early rule for a Shaivite ascetical sect called the Pashupatas. Although
their level of organization was still fairly rudimentary, the Pashupatas
pursued a course of training in several stages, based on Patañjali's
(c. 100) *Yoga Sutras.* Beginning with a simple initiation, the aspirant
went through a period of secluded probation and austerity. Returning to
society, the aspirant was to conceal his religious identity and act in such
a way as to bring scorn upon himself, proving he no longer cared for

social status. Finally, after six months of further training in yoga while in solitude, the Pashupata spent the rest of his life alone, devoted to following the example of Shiva the ascetic.

Tradition recognizes the famous theologian Shankara (788–820) as founder of the first major order, establishing monasteries in sacred cities at the four cardinal points: Badrinath in the north, Shrinagar in the south, Puri in the east, and Dvaraka in the west. Ten sub-orders of sannyasis, called *dashanami* ("ten names"), developed. Followers eventually established other autonomous foundations, in a pattern not unlike that of the Benedictines. Shankara's order was Shaivite, but a number of later Vaishnava orders were founded, beginning with that of Ramanuja (c. 1017), another renowned theologian. Shankara's monks learned the nondualistic Vedanta system of thought, with its mysticism of knowledge. Later orders incorporated more theistic devotional practices and appealed to a wider public. Orders founded by Nimbarka (c. 1162), Madhva (1199–1278) and Vallabha (c. 1500) were famous for their devotion to Krishna. In modern times new orders have continued to appear. Vivekananda's (1863–1902) Ramakrishna Mission marked a departure from tradition with its emphasis on missionary activity to spread knowledge of Vedanta. Other recent foundations in India continue the tradition of a settled monasticism whose doors are open to those in search of spiritual guidance or brief retreat. Famous founders include Shri Aurobindo Ghosh (1872–1950) and Mahatma Gandhi (1869–1948).

Living mostly in urban monastic foundations called *maths,* attached to temples, monks of the various orders wear distinctive garb and follow a daily regimen of prayer and meditation. Members may join for a time and then leave in the normal course of things. Internal structure in some orders reflects the four life-stages of traditional lay Hinduism: students are monastic novices; householders are those who maintain family life along with monastic affiliation; forest dwellers are those who opt for an initiation to a more strictly ascetical mode; and renunciants are those who vow perpetual celibacy and will remain in the order for life. Through the centuries, monasteries have maintained religious sites and traditions of religious scholarship, while supplying many social services to the public, including guest facilities for pilgrims, medical dispensaries, and Sanskrit schools.

MAJOR SCRIPTURES

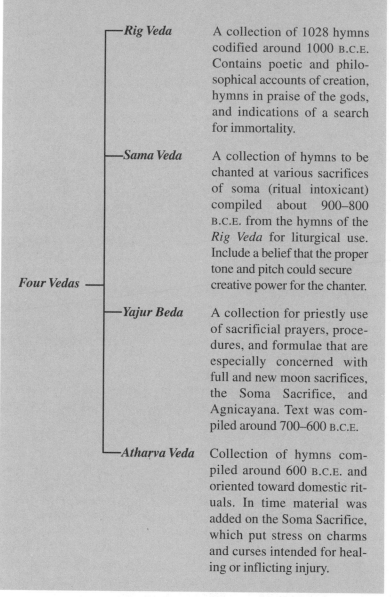

Four Vedas

Rig Veda — A collection of 1028 hymns codified around 1000 B.C.E. Contains poetic and philosophical accounts of creation, hymns in praise of the gods, and indications of a search for immortality.

Sama Veda — A collection of hymns to be chanted at various sacrifices of soma (ritual intoxicant) compiled about 900–800 B.C.E. from the hymns of the *Rig Veda* for liturgical use. Include a belief that the proper tone and pitch could secure creative power for the chanter.

Yajur Beda — A collection for priestly use of sacrificial prayers, procedures, and formulae that are especially concerned with full and new moon sacrifices, the Soma Sacrifice, and Agnicayana. Text was compiled around 700–600 B.C.E.

Atharva Veda — Collection of hymns compiled around 600 B.C.E. and oriented toward domestic rituals. In time material was added on the Soma Sacrifice, which put stress on charms and curses intended for healing or inflicting injury.

Upanishads The divinely inspired philosophical and mystical writings that comprise the closing part of the Vedic literature. Major themes include, 1) the identification of *Brahman* and *atman;* 2) rebirth *(samsara)* is contingent on one's action *(karma);* 3) liberation *(moksha)* comes through detachment from this world; and 4) the way to moksha is through meditation *(dhyana)*. Compiled around 500 B.C.E.

Bhagavad Gita "Song of the Lord." A conversation found in the *Mahabharata* between Arjuna and Krishna on the battlefield of Kurukshetra that has as its main theme the disinterestedness that is required in the performing of one's duties. Compiled about 200 B.C.E.

Puranas "Stories of Old." Legendary and mythological versions of creation, the history and destruction of the world, and other topics. Accounts emphasize the *tri-murti,* the Hindu "trinity" of Brahma, Vishnu and Shiva. Began as stories of edification especially for the lower castes and Women. Texts stress *bhakti* and miraculous manifestations of divine grace.

MAJOR HINDU DEITIES

Vedic Period

Agni (god of fire & sacrifice)   Indra (god of sky & war)
Varuna (upholder of cosmic order)

Devotional Theism: Vishnu & Shiva (and consorts)

Vishnu (Lakshmi/Shri)   **Shiva**

The Ten *Avataras*   Terrifying Aspect   Gracious Aspect

Matsya (fish)   (Kali/Durga)   (Parvati/Uma)

Kurma (tortoise)
                                          [offspring of Shiva]
Varaha (boar)
                                               Ganesha
Nara-simha (man-lion)
                                           Skanda/Karttikeya
Vamana (dwarf)

Parashurama

Rama (Sita)

Krishna (Radha)

Buddha

Kalki

THREE:

DOCTRINES AND PRACTICES

22. What is the status of religious doctrine in Hinduism? Is there such a thing as a "Hindu creed"?

Diversity of belief is generally much less cause for concern and anxiety among adherents of the many subcommunities of Hinduism than it is for, say, Christians and Muslims. On the contrary, Hinduism's variety and seemingly infinite expansiveness seem to be among its chief glories. Not that there are no sectarian Hindus who regard members of other communities of faith and practice as misguided, or worse. Nor do I mean to suggest that Hindu beliefs are merely amorphous and that one can believe virtually anything that strikes one's fancy. But the vastness of Hinduism's mythological patrimony, along with the historic tendency to subsume new developments into an ever-burgeoning organic whole, set Hinduism apart from other major faith traditions with respect to the role of doctrine. There are, to be sure, "doctrines" characteristic of different segments of Hindu society, such as the teaching of the unity of Brahman and atman; but one rarely finds universal acknowledgment of such notions, particularly the more abstract ones.

What then, if anything, functions as a control mechanism within Hindu belief systems? Is there any natural dynamic in the faith of ordinary folks that gives definition and shape to what they actually believe? I believe the concept of the "chosen deity" *(ishtadevata)* plays just such a role in a general way, providing the basic elements of structure and internal consistency that the more evident creedal formulations and doctrinal systems of traditions like Christianity and Islam afford. What keeps the daily faith of most Hindus from getting lost in the almost infinite number of divine manifestations or name-forms is their choice of one name and form over others. What guides this "preference" for most people is more than likely their immediate religious heritage: people grow up with a tradition that emphasizes one central set of narratives about the deity. Reflective, educated Hindus understand that the names and forms of their "chosen deities" represent a way of acknowledging the fullness of divinity within the limits of conventional language and symbolism. They are a means of expression that one must not mistake for the realities they seek to express.

An ancient tradition has it that there are 330,000,003 deities—one for each individual Hindu. Herein lies an implicit acknowledgment that however much human beings try to talk the same language about the ineffable, we invariably end up creating God in our own images anyway. Ask a co-religionist what he or she *really* means—in very personal terms—by the word *God,* and I suspect that this sort of Hindu God-talk will not seem so strange. Does all this mean that there is no such thing as correct belief among Hindus? Not quite. It merely suggests that there is no institutional machinery for monitoring and legislating orthodoxy, and that as a result, unanimity of belief occurs locally rather than universally. One gets the sense that beneath it all lies the awareness that, first, our language and symbols are inadequate to the task of bringing the divine down to within reach of our capabilities, and second, that God will always accommodate to our inability to handle more than a piece of the truth at a time.

23. If you had to choose just one concept or term to characterize Hinduism, what would it be?

Of the several that come immediately to mind, *dharma* wins in a photo-finish over *moksha* (liberation), *karma* (action), and *samsara* (cycle of rebirth). *Dharma,* from the root *dhr* meaning "to found, maintain, uphold," is perhaps the most fundamental and widely known concept, one so important in Indian society that it carried over, with significant reinterpretation, into Buddhism. The term has had several levels of meaning through its long history, functioning in modern times as a rough parallel to the English term "religion." Among its earliest meanings was the pervasive order in the universe, related to the Vedic notion of *rita,* and the word "ritual." As the unshakable basis of reality, *dharma* came, by a series of associations and extensions, to refer to all of reality as it is and ought to be, from the cosmic scheme to the most minute individual responsibilities. Eventually some theologians would appeal to the concept of eternal, unchanging *(sanatana) dharma* as ruling out any new teaching or innovative religious thinking.

Even the gods take account of Dharma when they act. From a metaphysical point of view, human beings have no direct input into the cosmic order of things; but in a more practical way, human survival depends on the choice for or against Dharma. To live according to the all-encompassing Dharma is to choose habitually those options the tradition has prescribed as "dharma" (with a small "d"), from acknowledging the duties of one's social station to proper performance of ritual to fulfillment of one's individual family responsibilities. In other words, the individual's righteous actions (dharma) in accord with the larger order (Dharma) assure one's place in the overall scheme of things.

An engaging story from one of the Puranas illustrates the centrality of dharma. One day a Brahmin named Gautama met a Vaishya (middle class merchant) named Manikundala. Gautama suggests the two search together for riches, for one can never have enough wealth. Gautama had overtly decided to swindle Manikundala along the way. As they go, they discuss the meaning and value of Dharma. Gautama plays the devil's advocate, arguing that *adharma* (denial of Dharma) is the best way to live—the author of this popular form of religious literature is taking a poke at the priestly class—and Manikundala counters that Dharma alone is a worthy goal. When they meet a stranger, they ask him to adjudicate their wager, and the passerby rules in favor of the Brahmin. Surrendering all his money, Manikundala is undeterred and decides they should bet their arms. Another passerby gives Gautama the nod, whereupon the Brahmin cuts off the merchant's two arms. Still undaunted, Manikundala bets his two eyes on Dharma. Again a stranger rules in favor of the Brahmin, who gouges out Manikundala's eyes, reviles him, and abandons him on the bank of the Ganges, near what happened to be a sacred spot. A king from Lanka (Sri Lanka) comes by, finds the poor merchant and heals him with herbs growing nearby. Very soon a blind girl wanders along, promising a kingdom to anyone who can heal her. Manikundala produces the herbs, restores her sight, and is instantly wealthy. Not long afterward, the merchant happens upon a now penniless Gautama and with great compassion takes him in. Dharma is both in the details and infinitely beyond them.

24. What are the most important traditional Hindu views on the origin and structure of the universe, of physical reality?

Traditional Hindu teaching on how things came to be as they are does not distinguish neatly between physical and spiritual realities as such. In Hinduism as in other traditions, "creation" stories are vehicles for describing the meaning that accompanies or underlies appearances. Hinduism's narratives and early speculation about how the cosmos came into being emphasize the sacrality of the universe. A unifying thread through its religious literature from the Vedas to the latest Puranas, Hinduism's creation imagery includes virtually every major metaphorical type, except perhaps that of the kind of "creation from nothing" central to Abrahamic cosmogonies (Judaism, Christianity, and Islam). The main theme within that thread, so to speak, is the conviction of the sacred origin of all things.

I mentioned earlier the arresting Vedic image of the cosmogonic dismemberment of the Primal Person *(purusha)*. Other Vedic metaphors for cosmic origins reflect on breath, water, and the heat generated either by an ascetic's self-discipline or a brooding hen as possible generating causes. Related to the last image is that of the "golden germ" or embryo, the primal egg that contains all reality including the gods. Later sacred texts further develop these images and add a few more. In the Upanishads, the egg splits into the silver (whites) of the earth, the gold (yolk) of the sky, the outer membrane of the mountains, the inner membrane of the clouds, and the veins that became rivers. Elsewhere in the Upanishads is the metaphor of sexual reproduction, whereby the One, feeling lonely, divides into male and female halves. The two give birth to humankind, but in shame at the incest the female tries to hide. She becomes a cow, but the male becomes a bull; a mare, and the male turns into a stallion; a she-goat, and he into a billy goat. Finally, she has nowhere to hide, but by then all things have come into being. This last image also clearly taps into the desire to know the primal origins of the incest taboo and the shame properly associated with it.

Popular religious literature continues the theme of how the world came to be. In a time before time, Vishnu the all-pervader lay at rest on Shesha, the serpent of endless time, floating on the waters of eternity. From Vishnu's navel grows a lotus, and as its petals unfold, Brahma the creator god emerges and creates the world. Vishnu awakens to rule for one "Day of Brahma," and as he sleeps a night of similar duration, he reabsorbs the cosmos into his body, so that the process can begin again. One of the more popular related myths is that of the Churning of the Sea of Milk. One variant begins with a moment in the endless contest between gods and demons, when the evil ones have gotten the upper hand and the deities are dispirited. The more clever gods persuade the demons to help them churn the sea of milk in order to make butter (though their actual goal is to raise the golden nectar of immortality from the depths). When Vishnu agrees to become the tortoise Kurma who will dive to provide a base, they use Mount Mandara as a churning stick, with Shesha as their rope with which to oscillate the mountain. Up from the deep come the "fourteen jewels" that are the prototypes of all things, preceded by a world-threatening dark cloud of poison, which Shiva ingests to save the world. Sun and moon, the goddess Lakshmi, and all living things rise in the cosmic butter. At last the golden nectar pot floats up. To distract the demons while the gods drink the nectar, Vishnu becomes a beautiful woman. But the demon Rahu, alert to the ruse, disguises himself and joins the gods. Vishnu kills Rahu, but not before the demon manages to quaff enough elixir to immortalize his head. To this day, the demon's head manages to compete with sun and moon by causing eclipses.

Scores of other marvelous mythic narratives bring out the same basic message of the underlying nature of reality without pretense at what we would call scientific explanation.

25. Is there anything in Hindu belief analogous to the Christian concept of salvation?

To the general notion of salvation as a form of liberation, yes; to the concept of being saved by divine redemption, no—at least not in the same way and not until the appearance of the *Bhagavad Gita*. Hindu tradition recommends as the highest goal of human striving the experience of *moksha* (or *mukti*), definitive freedom from the meaningless round of action-driven rebirth known as *samsara*. Moksha is the one life-goal to which one can aspire without tincture of ulterior motive, the only thing a human being is capable of wanting purely for itself. Pleasure *(kama),* wealth and status *(artha),* and even Dharma itself (as just discussed), the most sought-after of goals, remain bound up with ulterior motivation and cannot remain ends in themselves.

But what more precisely is the predicament from which human beings can seek emancipation? Even as early as the Vedas one discerns hints of the notion that human beings are of divine origin and that there is an animating principle, called *atman,* capable of existence apart from the body. But the solution to human problems was still considered in the hands of the deities, whom devotees could cultivate through proper ritual action *(karma)*. The Upanishads further identified the "self" with the larger spiritual reality called Brahman and replaced the fire of physical sacrifice with the inner fire of a knowledge purified of the illusion of duality. Through a process of experiment and elimination the seeker could approach an understanding of the true self and of Brahman, ultimate reality. Liberation in this view means freedom from ignorance. Well and good, and persuasive in its way, but very austere and demanding. What about the majority of people who naturally identify self with physical existence and hence with action?

One key is to understand the nature of karma and how one's own motives affect the quality of action. According to the law of karma, the effects of actions become attached to one's "self" *(atman)* and must be stripped away. In other words, the results of action are like a spiritual substance that entrap the self in the body. But since liberation from the temporary abode of the body is the goal, and it is only by transcending selfishness that one can achieve that ultimate destiny, persons who are bound to their bodies through their actions will experience another incarnation, with another chance to live a life in touch with the ultimate reality. The way to the cessation of the cycle of rebirth according to the *Bhagavad Gita,* for example, lies in learning to perform all one's actions without egotistical concern for their fruits, by living out one's own share of Dharma purely because it *is* one's Dharma. But that level of detachment is still very rare and difficult. Popular devotional Hinduism of the epics and puranas therefore adds an ingredient in the interest of making all of this a bit more accessible: help is available in the form of love and grace if one will only surrender totally to one's chosen deity in selfless devotion known as *bhakti* (literally, "participation"). Hindu soteriology remains very different from salvation by redemption. God's grace simply neutralizes sin and the evil effects of *karma.*

26. Given that view of human life, is there any room in Hindu thought for sacred history as Jews, Christians, and Muslims might think of it?

It is commonly observed that "Western" views of time tend to be linear, while "Eastern" views are more cyclical, but that does not characterize the differences satisfactorily. There is linearity in Hindu views of time, but the trains of events Christians and Muslims generally think will happen only once and yield permanently to timelessness, Hindus simply allow in multiples. There seems to be a theological foundation to this in that, just as Hindu thought has jealously protected its sense of divinity from being diluted by identifying God with any one image, so the notion of creation as an unending process keeps God from the contamination of involvement with time. Each segment in each cycle of "historic" time is unimaginably long according to the Hindu view.

Stretching the concept of time still further, Hindu tradition says that even the creator god Brahma has a fixed span (for any conceivable being cannot be the Ultimate Reality), and each day in this deity's life is equivalent to one thousand times the whole of human history. Human history, called a *kalpa,* in turn is divided into four ages, or *yugas,* of a descending duration that represents cosmic and moral entropy. The Krita Yuga was an age during which all was well and in order, when Dharma stood on four legs, there was no caste, and humans lived four thousand years. During the Treta Yuga, Dharma diminished by a fourth as did the life span of each human, the Vedas multiplied to four and communities of belief multiplied. Sacrifice, pestilence, and caste began in the Dvapara Yuga, as did sexual procreation. We now live in the sixth millennium of the Kali Yuga. In a bit over 400,000 more years, Vishnu will appear in his tenth avatara and bring the world to an end.

The four yugas together are called a *mahayuga* (great yuga), one thousand of which equal a day of Brahma, and the deity will live one hundred years thus. The present Brahma will die in a cosmic conflagration that will be followed by another period of chaos as long as one Brahma life. And the whole process will start over. Hindu tradition does have a notion of sacred history that even includes certain apocalyptic elements; but, like the greatest of the deities, it is potentially limitless.

27. Could you sum up the prevalent Hindu views of "the last things"? Is there a concept of any sort of afterlife in another realm?

Even in the midst of all the complex Hindu notions of samsara and endless ages of time, concepts of judgment, heaven, and hell survive in popular lore along with the more obvious reality of physical death. Body is only temporary, but the spiritual self lives on and will be held accountable for all choices. When we pass on to the next world for judgment, Yama, lord of the nether regions, tallies the individual's record and assesses reward or punishment. Perfectly sinless individuals are led upward to the paradise of Brahma, there to remain eternally. Those of less than pure virtue still ascend but enjoy a somewhat diminished bliss. Heaven for them is a temporary stop en route to another embodied life at a higher level than they had previously enjoyed.

These heavens are only two among many, and each more or less discrete realm is further divided into regions, perhaps not unlike Dante's various circles or the seven levels of classic Islamic narratives. Mythic tales describe each level's distinctive landscape, with sacred mountains, trees, and, of course, rivers. In sectarian lore, virtually every major deity has a unique heavenly realm, and myths typically describe the paradise of each community's chosen deity as a notch or two above those of the others.

For individuals judged wanting in their most recent lives, something less pleasant awaits. People who gave in to serious sin, but not without some struggle to ward off temptation, will taste purgation in one of the uppermost of the seven major hells. There they will be cleansed sufficiently to allow them a reasonable hope of improvement during their next embodied lives in states lower than before, depending on their degree of culpability. These hells function somewhat more like the Christian Purgatory. Individuals whose evil proclivities run so deep as to be irremediable are consigned to the lowest hells. Some theologians hold that such people will remain in hell eternally, not merely till the end of time, thus establishing a punishment parallel to the eternal freedom of the best of humankind.

For most people, heaven and hell are intermediate stops, lasting as long as the remainder of the current mahayuga. Death and judgment occur as often as each individual soul needs it on the long journey to freedom from rebirth.

28. What is the purpose of ritual in Hinduism? Are there many different types of rituals?

Hindu tradition encompasses perhaps the longest and most elaborate history of ritual on earth, beginning with the extensive catalogue of Vedic ceremonies alluded to earlier and continuing right down to contemporary adjustments required by changing social circumstances. The various overlapping types of ritual observance, known as a whole by the term *kriya* ("rites") in India especially reflect the enormous complexity of Hindu society. An extensive literature outside the category of sacred scripture, called Kalpa-sutras, contains the principal rubrics of ritual— the *shrauta sutras,* regulating rites of Vedic origin, and the *smarta sutras,* which govern those based on the later scriptures.

Rituals of Vedic origin, collectively known as *yajña* ("sacrifice"), have not altogether disappeared and still meet the need for a more generic way to address problems of fertility, assurance of the continued orderly processes of nature, and hopes for prosperity and power. Participants are in a way co-responsible with the deities for maintaining cosmic order. There is a consoling organic simplicity to these rites, oriented as they are to the primordial elements; they use temporary altars and use no icons of any sort; and fire is a customary requirement. Wealthy people still, but rarely, subsidize Vedic fire ritual or animal sacrifice on a large scale.

A more pervasive and popular category of ritual activity is called puja ("worship, adoration"). It includes a wide range of observances performed both in the home and in temples, differing from Vedic rites in that puja typically occurs at permanent altars (including smaller home shrines) and involves images of the deities. Offerings of simple goods, especially food and water, are essential to the interaction, though in some ancient temples puja still includes animal sacrifice. Home puja can include a daily round of observances, from special "auspicious" actions upon rising; to ritual bathing and oblation before breakfast; to special prayers for morning, noon, and evening; to attendance upon the deity in the home shrine.

Whereas the head of the household presides over home ceremonies, the priest officiates in temple puja, which may be either communal or restricted to the relatively private needs of individuals or families. When the deity worshipped is not the central deity of the temple, people may gather around the icon in an open part of the temple. If the deity is the chief, or one of the principal, divinities to whom the temple is dedicated, the priest alone may enter the dark "womb chamber," there to lavish devotion on the image on behalf of those waiting in the temple's congregational space just outside the inner sanctum. Chanting of prayers and scriptural texts are integral to temple puja.

Several other major categories of ritual are also important. Marking all of life's significant changes, from birth to puberty to special initiation to marriage to death, are the *samskaras.* Special rites associated

with the larger phenomenon of pilgrimage take various forms, depending on the sacred place that is the pilgrims' goal. And the practice of
yoga as a religious activity entails its own distinctive rituals.

29. Does Hinduism have anything like Christian sacraments?

Samskara, meaning "making proper, refinement," approximates a
Hindu parallel to the Christian term "sacrament." Hindu samskaras are
the various rites of passage that mark important transitions from one
stage of life to another. In general only the most traditional families still
manage to observe more than a few of the many rites. The samskara
cycle begins even before one is born, with impregnation and first
trimester rites in hopes that the child will be a son, and parting the
mother's hair in fourth, sixth and eighth months, in more immediate
preparation for delivery. Elaborate rituals attend childbirth, followed
about ten days later with the naming ceremony. In one version of the latter, parents write different names on two stones and place each before an
oil lamp. They then choose the name on the stone before the brighter
flame. Baby's first day out of the home, at four months, marks another
passage, including a ritual celebrating the child's first view of the sun.
Cutting of the hair sometime between ages one and seven, for both boys
and girls, and an initiation ceremony for adolescent boys (formerly performed between the ages of eight and twelve) are still common but generally not in their ancient forms. Numerous traditional samskaras mark
the various stages of a young boy's education, including his initiation to
Sanskrit and first reading of the Vedas. Rites of passage still most widely
practiced are those around marriage and death.

30. What are the most common Hindu funeral practices and ways of grieving?

A complex of rituals called *shraddha* marks death as the final samskara. Since mid-Vedic times, cremation has been generally preferred to
burial, but infants and revered gurus are usually buried. Let us assume,
for this example, that the individual dies in or near Banaras, as many
devout Hindus hope to do. Some families hire professional mourners
who encircle the corpse and send up sounds of lamentation. After wash-
ing, grooming and dressing the body the mourners, chanting divine

names, carry it to the burning ghats along the banks of the Ganges, led by the oldest son or senior male relative. With the body's feet being washed by the river, the family prepares the pyre; once it is kindled from the pot brought from the home, the chief mourner circumambulates it four times, keeping his left shoulder to the pyre. He pours clarified butter, called ghee, over the body as it burns, then pours the remaining ashes into the river, and the family returns home to begin a period of mourning and ritual impurity that lasts from eight to thirty days.

After the end of that period of inauspiciousness, the son prepares for the communal meal from which the rites get the name *shraddha.* Inviting Brahmin priests to attend, the son offers them, usually in connection with a larger dinner, specially made rice balls and then feeds the family and offers food to the deceased. Popular belief in the need to minister to the spirit *(preta)* of the deceased, to see that it is nourished and does not become a demon *(bhuta)* set adrift to cause trouble, remains widespread in India. Some people continue commemorative services several more times during the first year after death. The shraddha ceremony sometimes has overtones of a kind of seance in which the deceased is thought to be speaking through the principal attending priest. In any case, the net effect of the rite seems to be to secure ongoing auspicious relationships between living and dead. One index of the importance and complexity of shraddha is that ritual specialists have created for it a separate category of rubrical manuals called the *shraddha kalpa.*

31. Can you describe some regular ritual activities in greater detail?

Among the most characteristic groups of rituals is the *upachara* ("honor offering") service of the deity who presides over a temple or a home shrine. The governing idea is that the deity is a "person" whose image needs to be treated with appropriate respect, including all the nice things one might want to do for beloved royalty. Amid all the trappings of royalty, the deity enshrined in the home or temple has his or her regular round of daily activities. It begins when the temple staff (substitute here head of household for domestic purposes) wakes up the deity and clears away yesterday's flower offerings. In addition to the nightly rest, the deity may also choose to take naps at various times.

Bathing the deity comes next, sometimes indirectly, with the priest pouring water over the image's reflection in a mirror or using a nonrepresentational symbol for the deity, such as Vishnu's *shalagrama,* a small polished ovoid stone, or Shiva's *linga,* a smooth cylinder with rounded top. Many images are then clad in fresh garments. Worshippers then summon and welcome the deity, offering festive flowers and water for foot-washing or drinking. The centuries-old and nearly universal practice of circumambulation, either around the temple building or within a special ambulatory surrounding the womb-chamber but always with the right shoulder toward the sacred presence, precedes the formal presentation of gifts and entertaining the deity by waving bright lamps rhythmically before him or her. At certain times devotees will put forth more elaborate offerings of food prior to asking for what they most need or desire. The day ends with the worshippers bidding farewell to the deity, who then returns to splendid solitude.

At some temples the staff regularly take the image out for a stroll, and on major holy days they may carry a special processional image of the deity through the town or neighborhood. Throughout these ritual activities, an overriding goal of worshippers is to be granted *darshan,* to see and be seen by the wide-eyed deity who notices each devotee's desires and needs. Darshan is central to Hindu culture, and disciples of revered teachers seek darshan from them as they do from the deities.

32. What are some of the principal religious festivals of Hinduism? Do Hindus follow anything like a "liturgical calendar"?

Unlike many other traditions, Hindus observe no set day of the week as holy, for each day has its sacred possibilities. Religious festivals can be reckoned on both solar and lunar calendars, for practical purposes, but the lunar is preferred. To keep certain festivals occurring during the same season each year, an additional lunar month is added about every three years, thus making up for the shorter duration of the lunar year. Each lunar month has bright and dark halves, in relation to the waxing and waning moon. Some numbered days of the month are more important than others, yielding a total of 125 special days a year. For example, the fourth day of each half-month is Ganesha's, the eighth Durga's, the eleventh Vishnu's, and the thirteenth Shiva's. Not everyone celebrates all of the days, of course—Vaishnavas, for example, might not observe times devoted to Shiva and related deities—but there are plenty of possibilities.

There are in addition a number of major festivals. Krishna's birthday falls in July or August, with a week of musical performances followed by a special worship at midnight of the seventh day. Events of Krishna's life are commemorated in different rooms of the house. Only the strictest Vaishnavas refrain from celebrating Ganesha's birthday, in an ancient harvest festival that falls in August or September. In September or October fall the "Nine Nights," during which some fast in honor of Brahma's consort Sarasvati, others in honor of Shiva's consort Durga, Slayer of the Buffalo Demon. Feasting breaks the fast at the end.

Perhaps the most widely known of popular festivals is Divali (or Dipavali, "row of lights") in October or November. It is actually a series of five festivities, including one in honor of the goddesses Lakshmi or Parvati, one for Krishna's conquests of the demons Naraka and Bali, one for the reconciliation of Shiva and Parvati, and the middle night, on which Vaishnavites toast Lakshmi and Shaivites recall Kali's subduing her husband Shiva.

The range of acceptable manifestations of devotion is astonishing. On the feast of Holi, for example, indecent songs are common: it seems a demoness named Holika began eating a child a day, until a sadhu (a particularly holy renunciant) told a widow to gather all the children of the town and hurl vile abuse when the demoness approached. It worked. Other days are for gambling, drinking, or making vows, all depending on what mythic intervention is to be celebrated. All in all, the Hindu liturgical calendar is a marvel of color and variety truly befitting this "encyclopedia" among religious traditions.

33. I once visited a local Hindu temple and got the impression of a subdued chaos, with various groups of people apparently engaged in different actions, and no two people "on the same page," so to speak. Could you comment on that?

Hindu worship is generally not "communal" in the same way many Christians understand the term. It is true that large numbers of people may gather at a temple at a given time, but the mode of participation remains rather dispersed. A fair generalization about the difference between the way most churches, mosques, and synagogues function might be helpful here. Christians, Muslims, and Jews generally think of their places of worship as "houses of God" in the sense that they are facilities in which people worship and pray. Hindu temples are much more like "God's House," in that people go there as visitors or guests rather than precisely to gather as a community.

In most Hindu temples, individuals and family or other groups will typically move by turns toward one or another of the images around the temple. There they will enlist the help of one of the priests in making their offerings. The priest acts as a kind of intermediary, receiving the offerings of the worshippers, performing the actions that require direct contact with the image of the deity, and returning to the worshippers a token portion of their offering after the ceremonies. There are occasions on which groups of devotees will observe some ritual together, sometimes for a major festival prayer, sometimes for a performance of sacred music and dance.

Among individuals and groups awaiting their turn for puja, one often senses a festive mood. In a way that forms the communal dimension of temple worship. People arrive in expectation of joining together, not so much precisely in ritual unison, as in a shared participation in the divine *lila* (play). Many Christians and Muslims, for example, are used to thinking of primary liturgical worship as a generally subdued and serious affair, with perhaps a moment of levity sliding by here and there. For most Hindus, worship has a very different, more joyous and light-hearted, feel about it. That does not imply a diminished reverence and awe in the presence of the supreme godhead. It does mean that whenever Hindus approach the divine presence, they tend to do so in the conviction that God enjoys the whole business and wants human beings to share in the delight. What most Christians think of as God's "work," Hindu tradition prefers to see as God's play.

34. Is pilgrimage an important practice for Hindus?

Pilgrimage (*yatra,* "going") remains a major practice for many millions of Hindus in India, though most consider it a work of special devotion. Scores of important pilgrimage sites dot the map of India, each marking a sacred "crossing point" *(tirtha)* where the divine and the human meet. The Vedas do not call for pilgrimage as such; according to tradition, a ritual sutra dating from between 200 B.C.E. and 200 C.E. first decreed that all mountains, lakes, rivers, temples, and tirthas were capable of negating the sins of those who visited them reverently. In one traditional ranking of the five most important spiritual practices, pilgrimage ranks fourth, after meditation and piety, fasting and other austerities, and charity, and just ahead of concern for physical and mental purity. Long before the Hindu sources first mention pilgrimage prominently, a number of Indian sites had become pilgrimage goals for Buddhists. Buddhism exerted considerable influence on the development of Hindu iconography, and its pilgrimage practices may have had a similar influence.

There are several hierarchies of sacred sites, listed by category and usually in groups of seven—seven cities, seven rivers, seven confluences of rivers, seven temples—but these lists are by no means exhaustive. To these places, considered holy as a result of a theophany or by association with events in the life of a deity, pilgrims bring all their deepest spiritual aspirations. More arduous pilgrimages often include a full circuit of holy sites or follow a path whose periphery symbolically encloses a whole sacred sphere. Medieval pilgrims have become legendary for visiting all seven sacred cities during a single journey, for example. Devotees of Krishna still commonly do the sixteen-day, forty-mile "Vraj Mandal" around the deity's birthplace, entertained by a troupe reenacting Krishna's life story; or the six-day, thirty-six-mile circuit around Banaras. Pilgrimages to Rishikesh, site of the origin of the Ganges, and to the confluence of the sacred Ganges and Jumna rivers are also important. Every sectarian movement has its favored pilgrimage goals, specially trained social class of pilgrim guides, literature in the form of guidebooks that recount the pertinent lore, and rituals suited to each place.

Pilgrimages secure spiritual merit in proportion to the importance of the goal, the length of time dedicated, and the degree of physical austerity involved. As at Christian sites like Guadalupe in Mexico City, pilgrims en route to Hindu holy places sometimes up the spiritual ante by making the journey on their knees, for example. Rituals performed include a number of other ways of marking the spiritual transformation pilgrimage symbolizes: bathing in sacred water, circumambulation, shaving or cutting the hair, special marks associated with one's chosen deity, fulfilling vows, and the funeral shraddha when the mourners can arrange proper timing to coincide with arrival at a sacred site. Types of ritual are universal, but the tone and content (texts chanted, types of objects offered, and so forth) vary depending on the site and the deity whose presence makes it sacred.

FOUR:

LAW AND ETHICS

35. How are questions of ethics or morality decided in the Hindu tradition?

Hindu tradition has nearly always had a place for individual sages whose teaching and example have stood for the highest moral and spiritual values. Some of these teachers have even been revered by very large numbers of followers as special manifestations of divinity and therefore worthy of universal acclaim for their authority. Even when the authority of such teachers has crossed sectarian lines, however, it has not developed into anything like an institutional ground zero. Most Hindus would probably agree that Dharma is the universally applicable principle of order from which one must deduce all positive legal and ethical norms; and as I will point out shortly, one could argue that India's traditional and religiously sanctioned social stratification has in effect created a sort of central moral authority.

Before I get to that, a word about written sources that are at the center of these issues is in order. There has traditionally been very broad consensus about the authority of certain sacred texts in the Hindu tradition. First, of course, come the Vedas, but those earliest of scriptures have much more to do with ritual than with law as such. An important class of sacred texts in the larger category called *smriti* ("remembered") are the so-called Dharma Shastras or treatises on law. Earliest and foremost among those treatises is the metrical Sanskrit shastra ascribed to a legendary figure called Manu, dated around 150 B.C.E. Ancient tradition says that in its original form the code was much larger than later versions, steadily compacted by successive teachers. Since the Manu tradition descends largely from Brahmanical circles, many lower caste Hindus reject it altogether.

In its present form the Laws of Manu consists of twelve books. Beginning with a treatment of the origins of all things, Manu devotes the next five books to the duties incumbent on individuals as they pass through the four traditional stages of life, from student to householder to forest dweller to renunciant. Most of books three, four, and five treat the concerns of householders and their wives, since they naturally make up the largest of the stages in society at any given time. The second half of the work turns to broader issues. Books seven through nine discuss political implications, criminal sanctions, and the social ramifications of certain family matters. Saving the most difficult and abstract matters for last, books ten through twelve shift from legal details to ethical principles, concluding with a discussion of the relationship of action to the individual soul and prospects for ultimate liberation. Of special concern throughout the document is the maintenance of strict social order, with the Brahmin class calling the shots. Later refinements have codified particular laws differing from one state or caste to another across India.

Given the drift of the Laws of Manu and of subsequent dharma shastras and commentaries toward social control under the leadership of the priestly class, and the generally hierarchical structure of the caste system, must one not conclude that there is indeed a central authority in Hinduism? Broadly speaking, perhaps; but membership in the religious elite has been hereditary rather than a matter of institutional charter, as in the Papacy, or through special designation, as in the lineage of the Dalai Lama and other high lamas in Tibetan Buddhism.

36. What is the caste system and what are its legal and ethical implications now?

From early Aryan times (c. 1500 B.C.E.) comes evidence of a stratification of Indian society, with a priestly class at the top of a pyramid. Vedic hymns offer a theo-mythic justification for the origins of the system, and later treatises such as the Laws of Manu elaborate on the legal details. The four main classes or orders, called *varnas* (literally, color), were the priestly Brahmins, the warrior Kshatriyas, the merchant Vaishyas, and the peasant Shudras, a category by which the Aryans evidently designated all newly subjugated non-Aryan peoples. Probably already in place among the indigenous peoples was a structure based on the *jati* (literally, birth or species), a generally local group defined by occupation and language, and kept distinct by forbidding intermarriage with other jatis. By contrast, varna cuts across regional, occupational, and linguistic boundaries. Of the numerous jatis, numbering from two to four thousand by various accounts, plus over twenty-five thousand subcastes, some claim exclusive membership in one or other varna.

The Indian caste system is in effect a blend of the varna and jati systems, with the addition of a large population without caste or birth status, called "untouchables." Imagine the varnas as a series of concentric circles with Brahmins at the center. Within each of those circles, imagine the jatis as hundreds of discrete circles, some crossing varna lines. Over the centuries, certain duties and responsibilities have come to be associated with various social groups, so that each has its own *dharma,* according to a detailed codification begun in the Laws of Manu and amplified in later legal texts. Many castes have their own myths of origin as well as their unwritten taboos and expectations. Strict prohibition of intermarriage has kept the divisions very much alive.

Classical legal texts stipulate in amazing detail the behavioral expectations and sanctions for members of each major caste group. Some ancient codes clearly employ multiple standards and "sliding scales" in the assessment of guilt and reparation. To injure a Brahmin in any way brought the heaviest penalties, both materially and religiously; and virtually any individual of higher estate could mistreat or even kill a Shudra or lower-caste person with impunity. Caste is also intimately related to the Brahmins' ability to maintain ritual purity.

For practical purposes, the designations Kshatriya and Vaishya have largely fallen into disuse. And according to laws passed half a century ago, the caste system is now officially illegal. A system dating back millennia does not, however, disappear at the decree of a legislative body. As a result, many Indians still refuse even to associate casually with members of other castes. Divisions are so tenacious that members of Untouchable castes often prefer not even to be seen with members of other Untouchable castes. And the concern for contamination works both ways: an outcaste is just as likely to be offended at the thought of rubbing elbows with a Brahmin as the other way around. One cannot change caste except under most unusual circumstances, but violation of caste strictures can result in loss of caste affiliation altogether. Castes have sometimes moved up the social ladder by claiming their jati belongs to a higher varna than previously claimed. Caste structure varies regionally and is linked to village hierarchies. Increasing mobility of India's people has also caused considerable breakdown across the full spectrum of social order.

37. How does Hindu tradition classify ethical goals and acts? And is there a concept of sin in Hinduism?

Acknowledging the diversity of human insight and capability, Hindu tradition observes that people pursue a variety of aims in life, each with its value and purpose in the larger scheme of things. Earlier texts spoke of three goals: the pursuit of love and pleasure *(kama),* material gain and power *(artha),* and righteousness or virtue *(dharma).* When the Upanishads injected a strong note of introspection and began to question whether this-worldly goals were sufficient, the notion arose of two ways of seeking dharma—through action and through withdrawal to a life of contemplation. Thereafter, the fourth goal, of liberation from samsara *(moksha),* joined the list. Earlier texts seem to suggest these four are mutually exclusive, but some more recent Hindu authors have taught that what is important is to keep all one's goals in perspective by resolving to move eventually to the final goal.

One of the hallmarks of the Laws of Manu's view of the ideal religious life is the notion of four life stages. These cut across society in different ways, stipulating certain obligations for male members of the three upper varnas (Brahmin, Kshatriya, Vaishya). At an age established differently by each of the varnas, a young boy undergoes the initiation ceremony whereby he begins the student stage *(brahmachari).* Maintaining strict celibate discipline he studies the scriptures with his guru and learns service. In his later teens, perhaps, he marries the woman his parents have chosen for him and becomes a householder *(grihastha),* focusing on hospitality and upholding his caste responsibilities. Once his children are grown and have their own families well begun, he (and his wife) retire to solitude and a life of simplicity and recollection as forest dwellers *(vanaprastha).* Finally, at some unspecified time the man may choose total renunciation, seeking such freedom from material concerns as he can find in this world. Many renunciants *(sannyasis)* still walk the streets of India's cities, but the overall schema of the four stages has become a bit of religious nostalgia for most people.

As for the notion of sin, early scriptures have a strong but very nonpersonal concept of a violation of the divine order, in which an individual steps outside the bounds of established social norms or fails to perform proper ritual. One could cleanse the sin through further ritual and by admitting to the transgression in public. The sense of genuine moral, rather than physical or cosmic, evil begins to emerge in the Upanishads, but it is still seen rather as a failure in knowledge than a transgression against a personal divine reality. In the *Gita,* too, sin amounts to a failure of intention whereby one acts out of selfish or ulterior motives rather than a sense of duty. In the Laws of Manu, the beginnings of a sense of spiritual guilt and repentance appear, but still without distinction between intentional and unintentional misdeeds. With the rise of the popular spirituality of the Puranas and the devotional movements called *bhakti,* the tradition makes an unambiguous link between intention and moral evil, with the possibility of a salutary personal relationship to the deity. Meanwhile, at the moral fringes of the system, sannyasis and ascetics have all along established their own ethical standards by breaking the rules of ritual purity. They flaunt propriety by renouncing not only socially acceptable behavior but the very norms of conventional morality.

38. Has Hinduism developed any distinctive views on virtue and on the human person as moral agent?

One school of Hindu thought, associated with Shankara, holds that the core of the human person is the indestructible self or soul, called *atman.* The Hindu view of "soul" differs from some Christian theories in that atman is not only immortal but eternal, without beginning, and therefore one with the divine reality. Christian theories that explain the soul as "emanating" from a divine origin, however, are quite similar to mainstream Hindu views. Strictly speaking, identity of the self with the ultimate reality would mean that there is no individual self as moral agent. However, since the ultimate realization of the unity of Brahman-atman remains a relatively rare goal, Hindu ethical thinking retains a conventional language that acknowledges the average person as a more or less autonomous center of choice who must struggle to choose well.

In addition, traditional Hindu philosophical psychology analyzes the individual person as made up of the "three *gunas,*" qualities or characteristics that blend in varying proportions in each of one's actions. The moral goal of human life is to cause the more positive quality to predominate. Darkness *(tamas),* a bodily feature resulting from ignorance, tends to pull one toward laziness, indecisiveness, and sensuality. Goodness *(sattva)* is its opposite, bright and intelligent, and associated with the divine. Passion *(rajas)* is a form of energy from which the other two gunas receive their animation. Unchecked, heroic passion can lead to narcissism and blind ambition. The developmental task for the individual as moral agent is to refine his or her choices so that goodness predominates.

For practical purposes Hindu moral thought acknowledges that human beings need to have relatively proximate goals in order to keep striving. Markers along the road of ethical growth are the virtues (also called guna) and vices (the opposite, or *aguna*). Some of the earliest tallies of virtues included duty, compassion, noninjury, courage, truthfulness, nonacquisitiveness, and proper diet. More advanced qualities include asceticism, sexual continence, and renunciation. Finally, there is also the motivational notion that good choices yield spiritual merit. Even though in general the ideal is to perform actions without attachment to their fruits, when one acts with the ultimate purpose of liberation from samsara, the goal is no longer considered an ulterior motive but the one purpose worthy to be called an end in itself.

39. How does the individual become aware of his or her moral responsibility? How is morality taught at the more popular level?

Hindus have learned of their personal dharma most of all through family and closer social relations as well as through a vast tradition of popular lore. One's dharma is intimately tied to the norms of one's jati and varna as well as, formerly at least, one's station in life. An enormously popular epic called the *Ramayana,* attributed in its early form to Valmiki in the third century B.C.E. and evolved by various bards over the next several centuries, provides both a picture of a classic role model facing serious challenges and an example of a type of Hindu ethic that takes the "short view" in the interest of keeping it all within reach of large numbers of people. Rama's story is that of a householder and the epic focuses precisely on the moral needs of that life station, leaving the ultimate goal of moksha largely out of consideration. Dharma is interpreted much more flexibly than in the Laws of Manu, and in the most general terms especially in relation to caste. As the story goes, Ravana, the demon king of Lanka, abducts Rama's wife Sita, and Rama must find a way to rescue her, undergoing numerous heroic trials along the way and, in the end, upholding the values of morality over mere tradition. Of the four goals of life, the epic emphasizes the desirability of love rightly understood, power and wealth rightly employed, and dharma as virtue and compassion. Here is a genuinely life-affirming ethic oriented to solving life's problems here and now, with heaven seen as an extension of the same happiness.

In the *Bhagavad Gita* (c. 100–300), which became part of the epic *Mahabharata,* the picture changes somewhat. There the warrior Arjuna confronts the classic Hindu ethical dilemma. Arjuna must either fulfill his dharma as a Kshatriya and fight to the death, or withdraw from battle rather than kill his own kin, as well as beloved teachers from whom he had learned dharma. Arjuna tells his charioteer, Krishna, that he has no desire to win pleasure, fame, and power if the price is killing his own. Krishna gradually reveals himself as divine, unfolding his teaching that one must always follow one's dharma and accept it without attachment to the fruits of one's actions. One must make decisions on the basis of long range truths, seeking liberation alone rather than worrying about short term ends. Whereas the *Ramayana* left out the fourth goal, the *Gita* leaves out the first, desire, in favor of moksha. The *Gita* answers the question of whether one can aspire to true liberation while engaged in activity by declaring that the nonactivity of the renunciant is not the only way.

Finally, there is a significant historical strand in Hindu ethics that suggests that the only truly ethical behavior is that which moves beyond considerations of good and evil, pure and impure. Tantric theory and practice, taking its name from *tantra,* "context," have often gone from more conventional morality to the other extreme in an attempt to move beyond fixation on the "I" as moral agent. The impure (meat, wine, fish, aphrodisiac grain, ritual intercourse with a forbidden partner) was included with the pure in order to relativize ethics and demonstrate that ethical norms fall away in the context of ultimate concerns. Just as the ascetical and yogic traditions went against the grain of Brahmanical concern for purity, so did the Tantric. This is by no means mainstream Hindu thought, but Tantrism has appeared and reappeared enough in the history of Hinduism to require mention, however brief.

40. Is the concept of nonviolence, noninjury, a distinctively Hindu idea? Did Martin Luther King, Jr., derive his views from Hinduism?

When physicians take the Hippocratic oath, they promise first of all "to do no harm." There the caveat functions as a sort of ethical minimum in the performance of one's professional duties. In Hindu thought the principle of noninjury *(ahimsa)* stands likewise at the top of the list of ethical virtues, but its implications are broader than in the medical oath. Ahimsa begins with the conviction that *all* life is sacred and extends to thoughts and words as well as to action. Given the widespread practice of animal sacrifice in Vedic times, it seems clear that "noninjury" did not became an important issue until at least Upanishadic times. If reality is truly one, what appears to harm any given individual in fact harms all. Even on the level of karma-based ethics, harm done to another eventually brings the harm of continued rebirth upon the agent. At the very least, one should avoid injury if only to avoid defilement and gain merit.

Both Buddhism and Jainism developed similar notions as well, some Jains prescribing it in such detail as to forbid even farming or breathing unfiltered air for fear of injuring the smallest of creatures. Some suggest that it entered Indian thought under Chinese influence. In any case, the concept appears as a requisite virtue in the Hindu practice of raja yoga, the first of whose eight stages calls for ahimsa in the control over one's actions. Today many Hindus are vegetarian as a result of their concern for noninjury.

For Gandhi, ahimsa also meant that human beings should strive to live as simply as possible, since overindulgence so often means that others must do without basic needs. Drawing on ancient tradition, Gandhi recast what had been a virtue often motivated by other-worldly concerns into a moral imperative with more immediate implications. Protecting the life, rights, and dignity of all, was incumbent on every virtuous person. Martin Luther King, Jr., was very much influenced by the thought of Mahatma Gandhi, who introduced the principle of noninjury into the arena of political action. King made passive resistance a hallmark of his struggle for civil rights, even though he never thought of himself as borrowing from Hinduism as such.

41. Some people call Hinduism a world-renouncing religion. Is that so? And does that have serious negative implications for social ethics?

Asceticism in various forms has been an important part of Hindu tradition for aeons. The fourth of the classical ideal stages of life is that of the *sannyasi* or renunciant, and its chief virtue is called "ignoring" or "letting go" *(tyaga),* a passive form of asceticism that presupposes the likewise passive virtues of ahimsa and nonacquisitiveness. Even these nonactive forms of ascetical virtue are a means to an end, however, a way of getting what one really needs by foregoing what is only superficially desirable. Ironically, Hindu tradition has evolved an entire subculture of asceticism based on a more aggressive pursuit of spiritual power called *tapas* (literally, heat). Several Hindu religious orders are known as sannyasin orders and devote specific attention to such practices. Outside the orders, some yogis and sadhus dedicate their lives to practices designed to withhold and store up all their affective and sexual ardor, with the ultimate goal of achieving extraordinary powers called *siddhis* as they move toward liberation.

Since this is all very exotic and intriguing, treatments of Hinduism and related subjects often give the impression that India is a nation of bearded, emaciated men in loincloths who sleep on beds of nails. In fact only a tiny percentage of Hindus pursue renunciation on so grand a scale. In addition to the sannyasin orders and high-octane freelance ascetics, several Hindu religious orders are known as *vairagin,* rather than sannyasin, communities. Their members strive for the virtue of *vairagya* ("absence of passion"), a way of living in the world while remaining untainted by its negative forces. Vairagya means absolute equanimity and holy indifference toward all aspects of ordinary experience, including sickness and health, suffering and enjoyment, acceptance or rejection. This is very much like the nonattachment early Buddhist teaching recommended to monks and nuns, for the Buddha had rejected the extremes of asceticism represented by the sannyasin ideal.

But the quest for the vairagin ideal still does not describe the vast majority of devout Hindus. To this great throng Hindu tradition recommends a more modest level of ascetical virtue called "equanimity" *(shama),* which presupposes a host of passive virtues such as even-temperedness, forgiveness, patience, self-control, and contentment, all far from the advanced forms of tapas and tyaga and even from the relative moderation of vairagya. In general, Hindu asceticism is a matter of disciplining the body, an instrument which, like a steed, needs to be trained and harnessed.

Most Hindus consider pleasure and wealth religiously worthy pursuits. In fact, important themes in the tradition suggest that one can succeed at self-denial only if one has first sought material success and the delights of a happy home life. If Hinduism were a pervasively world-denying tradition, there would be no extraordinary Hindu art and architecture, no great

literature and drama. One would sense only drab resignation among a
people who would have no reason to cultivate the power of ordinary kind-
ness and simple delight. Instead, India pulses with energy, its citizens focus
vast personal resources and resilience on the solution of social and economic problems, and Hindus the world over celebrate life as though it were
actually worth living.

42. What do Hindus think about suicide or critical questions in medical and reproductive ethics?

Since there is no official centralized teaching authority that speaks
for all Hindus, there is nothing like general consensus, except perhaps
insofar as civil law dictates it. One can however trace some issues historically to get some idea of how they have been resolved in practice. These
are, however, questions of enormous complexity that Hindus have
answered in every way imaginable over the millennia.

Various forms of religiously sanctioned suicide have roots in
ancient Hindu tradition, but none are countenanced, let alone encouraged, in modern times. Among members of certain sects, such as the
mystical poet-saints called the Alvars, suicide by drowning in a sacred
river was not uncommon. Some communities built on the practice of
severe asceticism recommended death by starvation as meritorious, but
these are extreme cases. Suicide as a form of self-immolation has also
been known as a protest against injustice and, as I will describe later, as
a now illegal practice once recommended to widows immediately upon
the death of a husband.

Hindu views on matters such as abortion and infanticide also have
ancient roots. Beginning in the Vedic period, religious texts explicitly for-
bade abortion and even stipulated that a husband may leave his wife if she
induces abortion. There has always been provision for terminating pregnancy if a woman's life is in jeopardy. On the other hand, Indian civil law
legalized abortion in 1972. Increasing availability of amniocentesis has
also brought about a rise in abortion rates among people who desperately
want sons and are willing to do without daughters. Female infanticide is
an ancient problem on many levels of Indian society.

New issues in reproductive ethics continue to arise as technologi-
cal resources grow. But since Hindu law and social ethics are based
more on example than on adaptable principles, there is a serious gap

between religious teaching and pressing dilemmas. Ancient caste practices and preferences often fill in the gap, and scholars struggle to locate
parallel issues in the tradition that might serve as bases for contemporary ethical reasoning. For example, there is a kind of precedent for sur-
rogate parenthood in the epic *Mahabharata*. One episode tells how the
son of a queen by a marriage other than her union with the recently
deceased king was asked to impregnate one of the deceased king's wives
in order to preserve the royal line. Similar practices have not been
uncommon. The same epic tells a curious mythic variation on the theme
of *in vitro* fertilization: after a troubled pregnancy a woman delivers a
nonviable embryo, whereupon a magician keeps it alive in 101 pots,
which eventually grow into a hundred boys and one girl.

FIVE:

SPIRITUALITY

43. I have heard of a distinction between "Prophetic" and "Wisdom" traditions used to characterize differences between the Abrahamic spiritualities and those of Asian origin. Any other helpful large-scale comparisons?

Historian of religion Robin C. Zaehner described the religious traditions of middle eastern origin as "prophetic" and those of south and east Asian origin as "mystical" or "wisdom" traditions. Prophetic traditions, he observed, emphasize the transcendence and unity of a God who works in and through history and who communicates a revealed message by means of historical individuals called prophets. These traditions, which include Judaism, Christianity, Islam, and Zoroastrianism, generally trace their origins to specific historical founding or paradigmatic figures (Moses, Jesus or Paul, Muhammad, Zoroaster). Wisdom or mystical traditions, such as Hinduism, Buddhism, and Taoism, stress inner experience and the realization of one's own spiritual nature. Zaehner argued that mystical traditions focus on divine immanence and tend to be metahistorical, in that God acts directly in the individual rather than through history and the traditions did not grow from the teaching of a specific founding figure.

Contemporary Hindu thinker and former president of India Sarvepalli Radhakrishnan (1888–1975) offers slightly more refined, but still quite general, cultural contrasts between "East" and "West." Eastern traditions, in his view, emphasize intuitive rather than rationalist thinking; focus on mystery rather than concrete entities that one can formulate in creeds; seek to refine deeper realization of the divine within one's consciousness rather than engage in critical theological discussion; cultivate individual meditative calm and self control rather than promote active communal service and humanistic development; and see truth as having many forms rather than having a single absolute expression.

Both Zaehner and Radhakrishnan point out important broad features of the variant religious and cultural traditions. But it is important to take their contrasts as very broad generalizations intended to suggest typical emphases. All spiritual traditions include enormous variety. If sweeping contrasts such as these are to be useful, one has always to become aware of the similarities and common features as well, in order to avoid the temptation of a tidy compartmentalization. All the major traditions have demonstrated amazing adaptability as they have spread across the map. Nearly half a billion people in the Indian subcontinent and southeast Asia are Muslims, and that is not simply the result of conquest and political domination.

44. What do you mean by the term "spirituality" in relation to Hinduism?

As an academic discipline, the study of spirituality is a branch of theology that draws on the insights of systematic and historical investigations while paying special attention to that elusive phenomenon called religious experience. I use the term "spirituality" to refer to the ways in which the Hindu tradition defines the central relationships between the human and the divine; describes how individuals and communities might best fulfill those relationships; and facilitates that fulfillment by providing practical methods of pursuing life's ultimate goal and of evaluating one's progress toward it. Highlighting the relational and experiential aspects of religious belief and practice, the study of Hindu spirituality seeks to understand what images of the divine, the self, and material existence the tradition proposes, and the range of possibilities open to believers in their spiritual journeys. Within the expansive phenomenon that goes by the name "Hinduism," there is enormous diversity and, therefore, many "spiritualities."

Textual sources for the study of spirituality in Hindu tradition include, first and foremost, the scriptures, from the Vedas right through the epics, puranas, and sectarian texts called *agamas* ("sources of teaching"). Add to that a large body of nonscriptural devotional poetry that embodies the intense longings of devotees of Shiva and Krishna in particular; and manuals on every aspect of spiritual teaching and practice, enough to fill whole libraries. Nontextual material also contributes a great deal. Architecture, sculpture and manuscript illustration are especially important ingredients in a well-rounded study of religious phenomena; but because of a long-standing textual bias in religious studies, scholars other than art historians are only beginning to pay serious attention to the visual data.

In its role as mapmaker for pilgrims, the Hindu tradition sketches out in word and picture a number of features of which seekers must be aware on their journeys across the landscapes of the spirit. Images of the ultimate reality, whether conceived of as personal or as cosmic, describe the goal of life, provide the overall outline of the map, and alert travelers about what kinds of signs to look for. Images of material reality, of its relationship to the ultimate reality, and of the nature of the self, fill in the terrain. But a map needs pathways and roads, and Hindu tradition provides these in the form of various "ways," each with its chief scriptural sources and spiritual disciplines. The principal *margas,* methods or pathways, are the ways of ritual and ethical action, knowledge of the spiritual reality beneath appearances, and personal devotion to a chosen deity. Finally, travellers need directional and distance markers by which to assess their progress toward the goal. These, too, Hindu tradition supplies in the form of spiritual teaching and wisdom about how to distinguish inauthentic from authentic values, how to know which paths lead to a worthwhile destination and which to destruction. Like the history of so many other aspects of the Hindu religious tradition, that of its various spiritualities is vast and rich.

45. What are the principal paths by which, according to Hindu tradition, one can achieve one's ultimate goal?

The four *margas* ("paths"), as they came to be classically formulated, represent a full spectrum of spiritual methods. They need not be mutually exclusive, and in practice some people may end up trying them all or even combining several. Some of the methods are especially associated with broad historical eras, but all four constitute the enduring spiritual patrimony of Hinduism and remain live options for contemporary Hindus. These margas are also sometimes referred to as *yogas* ("harnessing") in the sense that they are modes of disciplined spiritual practice whose classic formulation appears in the *Bhagavad Gita.* In theory, there are countless spiritual paths, one precisely suited to every level of personal ability, and Hindu theorists have expanded their lists accordingly. The following three are central.

Karma-marga, the way of action, originated with the Vedic ritual concern for a way to control the powers of nature. The Brahmanical priests saw a direct connection between proper ceremony and the order of the cosmos. Even after developments in religious thinking represented by the Upanishads began to cast doubt on the efficacy of such magical beliefs, the way of action remained an important spiritual option. But the meaning of the word *karma* had changed: in the *Bhagavad Gita,* Krishna reveals to Arjuna that action performed purely out of a sense of one's duty or dharma, with no thought of selfish gain, leads to spiritual fulfillment.

Meanwhile the increasingly sophisticated reflections of the Aranyakas and earlier Upanishads offered the way of knowledge *(jñana-marga)* as another option. This is a type of discursive knowing that leads toward an intuitive, unitive knowledge. The development of contemplative or meditative techniques called *raja yoga,* in connection with physical exercises called *hatha yoga,* is often associated with the way of knowledge. Some consider the way of yoga a fourth path. Wherever one locates these yogic techniques as described in later Upanishads and special sutras devoted to the topic, the goal is to achieve freedom from enslavement to matter and to the true self. But the way of knowledge was clearly not for everyone because it was so abstract and required a life of disciplined contemplation impossible for the vast majority of people. Perhaps there was a way to acknowledge the unity of Ultimate Reality while at the same time taking account of the experience of ordinary folk.

Theologians like Ramanuja (d. 1137) and Madhva (d. 1278) developed ways of understanding and talking about God that would make ordinary people aware of a more personal, even intimate, relationship between the human and the divine. The popular movements that make up the Way of Devotion *(bhakti-marga)* were the result of this new thinking. Epic and mythical literature presented images of the deities that evoked awe and longing and the desire to surrender entirely to the love and grace of one's chosen deity. All of these ways, and others as well, are still very much a part of the living tradition of Hinduism. For most people the Way of Devotion is the path of choice.

46. How do the various images of God or Ultimate Reality function in Hindu spirituality?

Hindu tradition provides a number of models for understanding how the various "name-form" *(namarupa)* descriptions of ultimate reality communicate a piece of the biggest truth of all. First, one can talk of

God or the Brahman as Ultimate Reality either with or without qualities or attributes. Acknowledging the fundamental truth that no one name-form can adequately encompass the divine reality, Hindu theologians speak of *nir-guna brahman* (without qualities, *guna*). This approach is associated with what is often called "negative theology," which holds that the closest one can come to describing God is to say what God is not. In its extreme form, negative theology insists that anything imaginable or conceivable cannot be the ultimate reality. The next best thing is to think of God as immovable, imperishable, immutable, unmanifest. This kind of theological discourse does allow a few positive descriptors to sneak in, but they are such abstract attributes as truth, knowledge, goodness, beauty, and being. Austere as it sounds, important Hindu spiritual teachings have developed around the idea of the Brahman without qualities, but they have attracted limited followings.

Acknowledging the equally basic truth that God allows human beings to "picture" the divine, Hindu authors also speak of *sa-guna brahman* (the Brahman with qualities). Devotees of Shiva and Vishnu, along with their various manifestations and female counterparts, and of the Goddess apart from any male image, fill their language and art with concrete images of God engaging in countless characteristic actions. Luxuriant verbal description as well as visual iconography are a natural consequence of this kind of thinking. Still, popular visual expression gives a nod in the direction of inexpressibility, even as exponents of *nir-guna brahman* allow abstract qualities into their discourse: so-called aniconic imagery, such as the abstract phallic *linga* of Shiva and the spheroid *shalagrama* of Vishnu, suggest that one can barely hint at the reality of God. These two ways of thinking about God, without and with attributes, represent something roughly similar to what is implied in the distinction between transcendence and immanence.

The German philosopher Rudolf Otto defined the Holy as *mysterium tremendum et fascinans,* the mystery both terrifying and fascinating. This definitely applies to Hindu spiritualities, which acknowledge God now as awe-inspiring, fearsome, majestic, now as infinitely attractive and lovely. All the deities have their dreaded as well as their comforting aspects. None combines these opposites quite as fully as Shiva, but since terror and warmth never fit together smoothly, each verbal or visual description naturally tends toward one or the other.

Another polarity in Hindu God-talk is the male-female gender

dichotomy. Virtually every name-form of the deity, from the Vedic gods
on, has masculine and feminine aspects. Early deities such as Indra had
consorts whose names indicated their male counterparts immediately—
Indrani, for example. Later mythic embellishments describe the consorts
as discrete characters with their own rich life stories. But perhaps the most
telling images are those of divine androgyny, as when a deity is depicted
as Ardhanarishvara ("half-woman-lord"), half Shiva and half Parvati.

Finally, eroticism and asceticism, enjoyment and austerity, comprise yet another intriguing feature of Hindu descriptions of God. These
two aspects are evident especially in the imagery of Shiva. The more
expansive kind of divine imagery suggests unlimited power and possibilities; the more controlled suggests divine otherness from the ordinary
and transcendence of the mundane. Here again, one needs both aspects
even to hint at the divine truth.

47. Are there distinctively Hindu views about sacred time? About sacred space?

Traditional Hindu thought abounds in metaphors for mythic time
and eternity. One evocative image says that the "earthly" time of humanity is how long it would take for a bird with a silk scarf in its beak to
wear away the Himalayas by brushing the scarf against the peaks once
every hundred years. The meaning of time in relation to perceptions of
ultimate reality varies from one school of thought to another. For example, in Shankara's interpretation of *advaita* Vedanta thought, Brahman is
both the ultimate principle and the only category. Time and space are
illusory in the sense that reality only appears to be parceled out as a
result of the power of *maya,* and we play along by going to great lengths
(pardon the pun!) to give precise names to all kinds of spatial and tem-
poral measurements. In several of the other schools of thought, time and
space figure as important metaphysical and cosmological categories.

From the theistic perspective of the devotional movements, sacred
time is the mythic time into which one steps when recounting narrative
stories of the deities, an eternal stream into which devotees are privileged
to set foot while they worship. Each retelling of the deity's story is a
renewal of the deity's time, for the story of a divine being is not subject to
the laws of mere historicity. Paradoxically, time is eternal, but sacred time
is eternity. Most intriguing of all perhaps is the association of sacred time

with sacred sound. As in classical Hebrew, so in Sanskrit, to speak a word is to bring a reality into being; though the sound itself dies, the reality it embodied endures. Sacred sound brings sacred realities into being. Finally and in a secondary practical sense, sacred time is that of the calendar that reminds devotees of the arrival of auspicious moments for worship.

Traditional notions of space, except in advaita Vedanta, include both position and direction or distance. It is significant that each of the name-forms of the divine is associated not only with special places—cities, features of the natural landscape, sites of special occurrences—but with a direction or "quarter" of the cosmos. Of course, in any given sectarian movement, the chosen deity rules over all the rest and the subordinate name-forms fan out over their assigned segments of the spiritual universe, under the sovereignty of the principal manifestation of divinity.

As a matter of religious practice, just as the liturgical calendar regulates the timing of daily and seasonal observances, detailed canons dictate the arrangement of ritual space and of the physical relationships of all participants, whether of flesh or of stone. According to the traditional Hindu view of human history, we are now in the fourth cosmic cycle, the *Kali yuga*. And from the perspective of spiritual development, both yoga and the ascetical traditions suggest a view of time as progress toward the ultimate goal of liberation.

48. What are some of the key metaphors in Hindu spirituality?

Many important metaphors are directly related to notions of sacred time and space. Mixed metaphors may pose a problem for ordinary written and oral communication, but not for the religious imagination in general and most definitely not for the Hindu tradition. With a name that means "riverism," Hindu tradition naturally talks a lot about life as a world of flowing water, or more precisely, about life as quest for a ford *(tirtha),* a place at which one can cross the river. Rivers purify and give life, but more than that, each river is itself divine, beginning with Ganga, who descended from heaven and whose fall to earth was broken when Shiva caught her in his tresses. Rivers are thus both the very flow of samsara beyond which all worshippers seek to travel, and the divine power that brings liberation. And life is the pilgrimage that brings seekers in hope of the tirtha.

Earth and all material reality is the body of God, as in the arresting

Vedic hymn of the sacrifice of the divine Primal Person *(purusha)*. India is one enormous shrine to the divine body, ever since a grieving Shiva carried the burnt corpse of his wife Sati over his shoulder, 108 (a sacred lunar number) parts dropping off as he travelled. The resulting 108 "seats" of the goddess thus sanctified the whole land. In addition the earth is the abode of God, from the heights of the Himalayas that symbolize God's grandeur, as well as the intended spiritual ascent of believers, to the depths of the cave that is the womb-chamber of every temple.

Creation is the sound God the musician makes, and the rhythm of the divine dance is its sustaining power. All that is, and all that appears to be, is the divine play *(lila),* emphasizing God's all-sufficiency. God does not need anything and so is utterly free and spontaneous. Only the divine purposelessness makes sense of any human quest for God, for any deity required to fulfill some plan is clearly less than a God. From Shiva the Dance-King to Krishna the mischievous child, God plays and the rest is history. Countless other metaphors run through both warp and weft of Hindu tradition; these few are merely an invitation to stay tuned for more.

49. Is there a Hindu tradition of mysticism?

Mysticism can mean so many different things that it is important to begin with at least a general definition. By mysticism I mean the experience, as reported by the subject of the experience, of a direct or unmediated encounter with the divine. Records of mystical experience can be of many kinds, from lyric poetry to letters and diaries to treatises, and need not always be couched in the first person. As in a variety of other religious traditions, so in Hinduism there are at least two broad categories of spirituality that one could call mystical. One is a kind of cosmic or unitive mysticism in which the experiencer discovers that he or she is not a distinct self, but rather one with a cosmic reality. The other is theistic or dualistic mysticism, in which the experiencer and the deity are perceived as separate; however intimate the experience, the mystic is aware of remaining him or herself through it, or at least of returning afterward to the state of individuality.

Scholars have described Shankara (788–820) as a prime exponent of unitive mysticism, often comparing and contrasting him with the Christian mystic Meister Eckhardt (1250–1327). Shankara's whole system of thought derives from his meditation on the Upanishadic teaching of the oneness of the Brahman (absolute reality) and atman (soul). For Shankara, attaining the knowledge of the complete unity of all reality is the goal of a long process of clarifying one's perceptions. Banishing the ignorance (literally, non-knowledge, *a-vidya*) that binds one in the snares of illusion, the spiritual seeker purifies all affections of desire for control and individuality. The language of unitive mysticism seems quite cool and detached, but it is not without its passionate longing, a yearning to be one with the Truth. In fact, Shankara recommended intense devotion to Shiva as an integral part of his teaching.

More explicitly, theistic mysticism of the latter sort is a major theme in Hindu spirituality. The Bengali saint Chaitanya (1486–1533) is an excellent example, though there are many possibilities from which to choose. A conversion experience when he was in his early thirties turned the successful teacher of logic and grammar into a devotee of Krishna. He promoted forms of communal spirituality designed to provide an atmosphere in which devotees could encounter Krishna. His followers likened him to the deity, much as writers about Christian saints like to point out parallels between the holy person and Christ. Chaitanya promoted a highly emotional spiritual path in which the devotee became one with Krishna through practices designed to release inhibitions and allow flights of ecstasy. In the midst of a life of strict asceticism and celibacy, Chaitanya embodied the myth of Radha's longing for Krishna.

Ultimately, one cannot draw a neat line between the two emphases or styles of mystical spirituality. Chaitanya's followers tell a story of how he won a debate with a follower of Shankara's approach. Shankara recommended devotion to Shiva and the various associated name-forms of divinity as part of the initial stages of spiritual experience. And the poet-mystics of bhakti are keenly aware, amid their intense devotion, that all their vivid imagery of the deity pales in the face of the all-encompassing reality it represents.

50. Does spiritual direction or guidance play any role in Hindu tradition?

As early as the Vedic period, the teaching *guru* came to be an important figure, passing on the revealed scripture to the young students who came to live in his house. Eventually, the role of the guru developed into that of a spiritual guide in one-to-one relationship with a disciple *(shishya or chela),* of the sort around which the Upanishads seem to be modeled. As the guru function came gradually to be a central institution in sectarian groups, teaching gurus were largely replaced by gurus who initiated aspirants into religious orders *(diksha gurus)* or passed on to disciples a religious chant related to the group's traditional teaching *(mantra gurus).* From a root related to the Latin *gravis,* "heavy or weighty," the term guru thus came to mean one whose special knowledge made him spiritually massive and thus a source to be sought after.

A guru's knowledge comes from personal experience and extensive psychic modification through yoga, so that the teacher is free from the pull of pairs of opposites like joy and sorrow, success and failure, sickness and health. A guru is, above all, truly detached. As a classic story makes clear, such detachment does not necessarily depend on having few possessions. It seems a certain monk was scandalized by a king's riches. Through his yogic powers, the king ignited a fire that raged through his palace. As the monk frantically grasped his bag and bowl for fear of loss, the king sat calmly. The moral: detachment does not mean renouncing much only to be enslaved by a little, but staying peaceful in the midst of whatever loss one suffers. Most of all the guru must break free from ego, the better to be devoted to the care of others.

Before accepting a disciple a guru must ascertain that the aspirant is familiar with scripture, has a strong sense of the difference between reality and illusion, has renounced transitory pleasures, is possessed of requisite virtues of patience and concentration, and most of all, has the keenest desire for spiritual freedom. The relationship begins with proper initiation into a life of intense devotion, often including the imparting of a secret, specially chosen mantra charged with spiritual power *(shakti)* targeted precisely at the disciple's unique needs. For the disciple, the guru stands in God's place, the infinite in finite form. When sin predominates, the disciple will regard the guru as merely human, but when virtue is ascendant he will consider the guru as Shiva or Vishnu.

Eventually, the disciple gains an appropriate sense of self and learns to discover the guru within. As a form of homeopathic therapy, the guru-disciple relationship induces a feeling of alienation, risking a temporary experience of apparent psychic disorder. Driven to desperation and surrender to the guru, and in the process of surrender of what is not authentic, the aspirant can discover the true self. Dramatic contemporary change in India, not only in the caste system but in society at large, has diminished the traditional role of the guru considerably, but *ashrams* continue to provide important services to many spiritual seekers.

51. Do "holy persons" in Hinduism mediate between the divine and the human? What about saints?

Although there are several categories of spiritual beings who possess holiness and power in Hindu tradition, none enjoy the "official" institutional stature of saints in Christianity. One important class of spiritual beings are called *pitri* (fathers or ancestors), a group that includes the primordial forebears of deities and demons as well as of humankind, and the deceased members of any Hindu's family. The latter are the most important; their ongoing presence is cause for concern, since they must be appeased. *Rishis* (sages) are like the primordial pitris in that they are largely legendary or mythical figures, but they nevertheless serve an important function. Sages are the sources of the ancient scriptures and wisdom traditions. Neither divine nor demonic themselves, the prickly and irascible rishis were often feared by the gods because of their ability to stir up trouble if offended.

Perhaps the best known equivalent of Christianity's saints are India's *sadhus,* men and women who have reached a level of achievement called *sadhana* ("gaining") characterized by enlightenment and supernatural powers called *siddhis.* Sadhus can be monks who reside in a monastery, itinerant mendicants who are either monks or lay persons, or lay persons noted for holiness and affiliated with, but not resident in, a monastery as members of a sort of "third order." Sadhus are sometimes not obviously renunciants and may live in quite ordinary external circumstances.

Most sadhus of course have been influential on a very local scale, but there have been scores of men and women whose reputation for holiness has secured them a place in Indian religious lore. People can become sadhus by choosing to do so, but it is a type of popular acclaim that confers on a select few the mantle of sainthood. Accounts of their lives and miracles are a relatively recent phenomenon, and few written sources survive from before about the sixteenth century. Every famous saint represents an embodiment of the deity to whom he or she was dedicated; some devotees revere their saints as incarnations of the deity. The line between divinity and humanity is often nearly impossible to discern. People pray to and worship their favorite saints, and many of the holy personages are even enshrined in temples alongside of the temple's principal deities. For Hindus, saints are part of the seamless fabric of sanctifying power and presence that forms the expansive context of their spirituality.

52. What is the meaning of the term "yoga" as it is popularly used now? I recently saw a flyer for a course in Kundalini Yoga—what is that about?

Many non-Hindus all over the world have taken up the practice of a regimen of physical exercises known generically as "yoga." Strictly speaking, these popular exercises are classically known as *hatha yoga.* As described in Patañjali's *Yoga Sutras,* there are eight *angas* ("limbs") in the discipline, and one works on the first five simultaneously. The limbs are, first, external control *(yama)* as in refraining from injury, deceit, stealing, sexual activity; second, internal control *(niyama)* involving serenity, purity and goal-directedness; third, proper position *(asana)* in which to perform further exercise comfortably and without distraction, along with various postures that constitute the primary goal for most practitioners of hatha yoga; fourth, control of breathing *(pranayama);* fifth, elimination of perception of external objects through control of the senses *(pratyahara);* sixth, and the beginning of the state of "single-pointedness," is concentration *(dharana)* on some symbolic object such as a flame, the heart, God; seventh, meditation *(dhyana)* in which the object of concentration fades away; and finally, contemplation or absorption *(samadhi)* of consciousness into unconsciousness in a state of total freedom.

Actually, much of what is taught as yoga in the non-Hindu world involves only parts of this progressive program. Moving beyond hatha yoga to *raja yoga* (royal or kingly) means achieving the basic goals with much more attention to the last four of the eight stages. Adepts are able to achieve the higher levels without ever addressing the physiological phases directly.

The term *kundalini* means "coiled" and refers to a type of energy believed to reside at the base of the human spine. Certain types of yogic practice are methods for awakening this power that is as dangerous as a dormant serpent. Properly disciplined, this energy is immensely beneficial and liberating; but without guidance it can unleash a demonic and destructive rage. Under skilled tutelage, practitioners seek to allow the kundalini energy to progress upward along the spine through a series of energy centers or "wheels" *(chakras)* symbolically imagined as lotuses. Moving the energy to each successive chakra sets free distinctive spiritual powers. The experience of "piercing" all six chakras is said to be exceedingly rare and accompanied by a kind of mystical ecstasy characterized by a host of auditory and visual phenomena.

53. Could you describe some common forms of Hindu vocal prayer?

In addition to the often splendid hymns of the Vedas, Hindus have devised numerous other forms of vocal prayer for every occasion. Perhaps the most familiar to non-Hindus is the *mantra,* now meaning a short formula of a few syllables though the term originally referred to the Vedic hymns themselves. A mantra is a phrase or sound assigned specially to an individual that allows the one praying to "become" the meaning of the mantra. It is a sonic embodiment of divine power, giving the one who pronounces it a connection to the eternally ancient wisdom of the sages. The sacred syllable "Om" is a kind of mantra by which one meditates on God; it is the very sound of Brahman in which all other sounds are contained. Its four "measures," take one from the waking state (the sound "ah") through the dreaming state (the sound "oo") through the sleeping state (the sound "mmm") to the true self (as the sound tails off into nothingness as symbolized by the dot in the Sanskrit spelling of Om).

Related to the mantra is *japa* ("muttering"), in which one murmurs or whispers brief texts or divine names that, said aloud, would be mantras. The idea of japa is to provide, much in the way many Catholics have learned to use the Rosary, a sort of controlled distraction, and in fact Hindu *japakas* often use beads to count as they pray. Both mantra and japa derive their words and their power from ancient sacred sources. Other forms of prayer, such as hymns, *bhajans,* and *kirtans,* are of human origin. Singing for liturgical and private purposes has long been important in Hindu spirituality. Using ancient song forms, devotional authors have composed countless expressions of longing and pleas for forgiveness. The *bhajan* is a song, usually accompanied with percussion, strings, and dancing, that pours out the devotee's love for God, usually Krishna.

The *kirtan,* as it is called in Bengal, can either repeat names of God melodically (as in "Hari Krishna, Hari Rama, Hari Krishna, Hari Hari") or tell a story of what God has done.

54. Some of the temple sculptures I saw during a trip to India seemed frankly erotic. Is sexual imagery a significant religious theme?

Let me begin with two preliminary observations. First, sexual imagery is not necessarily erotic imagery, although if you saw the temples of Khajuraho, "frankly erotic" is an apt description. Sexual imagery tends more toward metaphorical expression of powers of fertility and creativity, whereas erotic imagery tends to focus more explicitly on sexual activity as an end in itself. Second, all the devout Hindus I know place a high value on modesty, some to such an extent that they are offended even by the suggestion that the Shiva-linga is a symbolic phallus and a sign of the deity's infinite potency. Similarly, many Catholics would be shocked at the suggestion that there is sexual imagery in the ancient Easter ritual of dipping the giant candle into the baptismal water. Neither is an instance of erotic imagery, however.

There is no getting around the fact that the aniconic symbolism of the linga, the love story of Krishna and Radha, the cavorting of Shiva with Mohini, the monumental eroticism of the temples of Khajuraho and Minakshi, and so many other expressions of Hindu religiosity over the centuries, deal with sexuality quite openly. Along with others, I should say rather that these expressions "use the *imagery* of sexuality," since the stories of the deities are not primarily about sexuality, but rather about realities so profound that only the use of striking, even shocking, metaphor will approach the truth. However one puts it, the fact remains that mainstream Hindu religious myth, lore, and art speak the language of sexuality more freely than almost any other tradition. Great mystics of nearly all traditions sometimes resort to romantic and sensual imagery; the Song of Songs is surely among the world's amatory classics. But the religious classics of Hinduism celebrate the spiritual beauty and potential of human sexuality in ways that go well beyond the purely mystical.

Most of the imagery is clearly metaphorical and in no way suggests that the devout Hindu should in any way engage in blatantly reprehensible practices. There have been, however, esoteric cults associated with Tantric ritual that have emphasized the transcendent nature of sexuality.

Tantrism is based on the conviction that human sexual union can be a means of enlightenment to the degree that one can imitate the cosmic order of natural harmony with such control that the participants do not seek simple indulgence. So prevalent were Tantric cults in eastern India for a solid half-millennium during the medieval period that its history makes no sense without some account of them. Many of the Tantric texts take the form of dialogues between Shiva and Parvati in which they discuss a range of conventional topics, from cosmogony to magical powers to meditation.

Clearly open to serious abuses, such esoteric cults represent what is for many Hindus a shocking, degenerate, and reprehensible aspect of Indian history hardly worthy to be included in a treatment of religious topics. I have included this brief mention here simply because the prevalence of related imagery in art and literature, and the obvious resonances all along the edges of mainstream Hindu spirituality, are such that one cannot merely sweep it under the rug.

MARGAS (SPIRITUAL PATHS)

Karma (action) The path to salvation through proper ritual and moral action (karma) as a means for attaining spiritual progress. Includes the purification of one's actions through a detachment from their fruits.

Jnana (knowledge) The process of attaining an intuitive or mystical understanding of the higher knowledge of reality, leading to an inner vision of the absolute truth; gained by meditation on the wisdom of the scriptures and traditions.

Bhakti (devotion) Devoting oneself to a chosen manifestation of the deity by making selfless service and emotional attachment to that divinity the core of one's existence.

Six:

Hinduism and The Humanities

55. Are there any schools of philosophy associated with Hinduism?

Six "views" *(darshanas)* or interpretations of the Vedas and Upanishads form the foundation of Hindu philosophy. Some were initially nontheistic but were eventually transformed into theistic schools, and together they have become the basis of all subsequent theological developments. Each is traditionally associated with a specific, if legendary, founder. Major texts of the schools are in the form of *sutras* ("aphorisms"), augmented by extensive commentary. Here are some of the most important features of the darshanas.

Kapila's *Samkhya* ("reason, discriminating knowledge") system (c. 500 B.C.E.) describes all reality according to twenty-five categories of matter *(prakriti)* and spirit *(purusha),* the two basic principles. Its purpose is to arrive at true knowledge by synthesizing into a unity all these various constituents, which by this time had become integral to Hindu ethical thinking. Over the centuries, theoretical Samkhya came to be paired with the more practical *Yoga* system of Patañjali, which added God as the twenty-sixth category. In this system, God, like all the other categories, functions as a focus of meditation.

Founded by Jaimini (c. 200 B.C.E.), a third system called the *Mimamsa* darshana departs from the other schools in its insistence that knowledge is insufficient for liberation. Ritual remains essential, even though the system did not originally require or presuppose belief in God. The principal contribution of Mimamsa is its elaborate system for interpreting the mysteries of the Vedas. Sometimes called *Purva* ("early") Mimamsa, the system has traditionally been paired with *Vedanta,* also known as *Uttara* ("later") Mimamsa. Sharing, in the Vedas, the same scriptural foundation, the two schools complement each other, Mimamsa focusing on the ritualistic Brahmanas and Vedanta on the more theoretical Upanishads. One could say their respective central principles are the philosophical equivalents of works (proper ritual) and faith (salutary knowledge).

Somewhere between the mid-fifth century B.C.E. and the first C.E., a philosopher named Gautama inaugurated a fifth system called *Nyaya* ("going into, analysis"). Based primarily on logic, Nyaya began as a nontheistic view that faulty reasoning is the cause of suffering and that one can arrive at the truth by correcting fallacious thinking. To root out errors in knowing, Nyaya analyzes reality into sixteen logic-based categories, thus offering a distinct alternative to Samkhya's more synthetic approach. Finally, Kanada's (c. 250 B.C.E.–100 C.E.) *Vaisheshika* school makes a natural partner for Nyaya because of its similarly analytical method. But Vaisheshika uses six categories to aid in realizing the incompatibility of spirit and matter. From pre-existent elemental substances, God created the world. Through analysis one arrives at the knowledge of the particularities *(vishesha)* of all things that alone can set one free from enslavement to matter.

These six are called the *astika* ("so-sayers," or doctrinally agreeable) schools. Other philosophical schools that have arisen in India, such as those associated with Jainism and Buddhism, are classified as *nastika* ("deniers or rejecters" of the Vedic tradition) views.

56. Has Hinduism produced any theologians comparable in importance to, say, Aquinas and Augustine for Christianity?

Hindu theology, like just about everything else one can associate with the tradition, is enormously rich and sophisticated. Three figures, Shankara, Ramanuja, and Vallabha, represent some of the most important developments. Many scholars refer to Shankara (788–820) as a philosopher, but his importance in the history of Hindu understanding of God suggests that he also owns a place among philosophical or systematic theologians. Shrouded in myth and legend, Shankara's life story begins with the tradition that just when his aging Brahmin parents were sure they would have no descendants, his mother became pregnant by the power of Shiva.

Shankara was a prolific author of commentaries on classic Hindu texts, such as the major Upanishads, the *Bhagavad Gita* and Patañjali's *Yoga Sutras.* But his theological significance lies chiefly in his refinement of the principles of "a-dvaita," or nondual thinking about Ultimate Reality. He taught that all of reality is an undivided unity, and that what we mistakenly believe to be personal individuality and material multiplicity are the results of ignorance and misperception. The goal of all religious seekers is to cut through the sludge of misunderstanding that threatens to keep them mired in endless rebirth, to arrive at a hard but bracing truth in which there is no room for the sense of personal identity human beings find so comforting. But Shankara tempered his theoretical idealism with a practical realism based on a theory of two levels of truth: along with philosophy, myth and devotion to Shaiva personifications of deity offer at least a glimpse of the higher verities.

Ramanuja (c.1017–1137) was a Vaishnava theologian who lived under the Shaiva Chola dynasty of south India. He taught that devoted love of God *(bhakti)* rather than knowledge is the key to liberation from the suffering that arises from lack of faith. He was the first to offer a theistic critique of Shankara. As his name suggests, Ramanuja taught that Rama was the highest of Vishnu's avatars. In his Sanskrit works, Ramanuja countered Shankara's nondual model of reality by asserting that ultimate reality is one, but is internally complex, not simply undifferentiated as Shankara taught. Individual souls are one in and with Brahman but are not identical with Brahman. Ultimate reunion with God does not mean loss of individuality, therefore, and Ramanuja's theology retains an attractive warmth hard to find in Shankara.

Vallabha (1479–1531) was also a Vaishnava of south India, but his theology revolved around Vishnu's avatar Krishna. He called his theology a "pure monism," arguing that although human individuality and the multiplicity one sees in creation are real, they do not dilute God's oneness because God, as Krishna, freely chose to create and thus become differentiated. At the center of Vallabha's theology is the notion that by playing and taking delight in creation, God bids devotees to revel in the divine abundance. The so-called "love games of Krishna," amorous tales of the irresistible attractiveness of God, provide the narrative around which Vallabha's thought develops. Modern interpreters of Vallabha have been especially cautious about how they "translate" his thinking, particularly in light of the excesses and unacceptable aberrations to which the sect fell prey during the eighteenth and nineteenth centuries. Teachers of Vallabha's school of thought tend to emphasize the need for careful metaphorical interpretation of the sacred texts, especially of the Puranic narratives of Krishna and the *gopis* ("cowherd girls").

57. Has literature as an artistic medium played a role in communicating central Hindu teachings and values?

Hindu writers have produced countless religious texts of high literary merit, and many of the most important works have been written in verse. Some prose treatises, mainly in Sanskrit, have developed elaborate theories of poetics and aesthetics that relate to spirituality. In order to give some sense of the breadth of Hindu literary tradition, I will mention only a few of the major authors and works of poetry in languages other than Sanskrit.

One major regional poetic tradition was that of the Alvars, Vaishnava mystics who lived in south India from around 600 to 800 and wrote in Tamil. Originally gathered in the tenth century as the "Collection of Four Thousand Songs"—revered as the Veda in Tamil—the poems talk especially of Krishna's dalliance with the gopis and Rama's heroic deeds. Critics proclaim Nammalvar (c. 800) the most accomplished of these poets, and devotees see in his poetry a distillation of the Vedas, even referring to one poem as the "Upanishad of the Dravidian people." Tamil first became a notable literary language in Tiruvalluvar's (c. 300–400) lengthy didactic poem, *Kural,* which reflects on a range of ethical issues somewhat like Biblical Wisdom literature or an extended Sermon on the Mount. The Alvars further refined the Tamil language as a vehicle of artistic as well as religious expression.

Another important regional tradition developed in Maharashtra state in west central India. Jñanadeva (1275–96) was among the earliest poets to raise the Marathi language to literary heights. His more than one thousand lyrics celebrated Vaishnava themes, featuring especially Krishna and Radha. One of Jñanadeva's chief disciples, Namadeva (c. 1270–1350) belonged to a whole family of poets and devoted his Marathi and Hindi *abhangas* (hymns) to Vishnu. Continuing the Marathi tradition into early modern times, Ekanatha (fl. 1560) was a scholar-poet whose work included careful editing of a major treatise by Jñanadeva. In the simple, direct imagery of his lyrics he spoke especially to outcastes and women, so that he became known as a champion of social equality in the face of an entrenched caste system. Tukarama (1607–49) was a Shudra devotee of Krishna whose simple hymns made him a poet of enduring popularity in Maharashtra.

A third major group were the Virashaiva poets of Tamilnadu who wrote free-verse known as *vacana* in a Dravidian tongue called Kannada.

Virashaiva devotion focuses on the "heroic" (*vira,* as in the English word "virile") or militant aspects of Shiva's power. During the heyday of Virashaiva lyric, from around 900 to 1100, four poet-saints produced a body of literature revered as the "Kannada Upanishads." The vivid imagery of these originally oral lyrics communicates with an arresting directness a wonderful sense of the color and intensity at the heart of bhakti.

These are only a few of the many significant developments in Hindu religious poetry, but enough to offer a taste from an incredibly rich table.

58. Growing up Catholic I've seen lots of religious art, but Hindu art is so different I'm not quite sure what to make of it. Can you offer any clues?

Catholicism and Hinduism both have long traditions of visual arts in virtually every medium, but the ability to appreciate the art of one's own tradition doesn't necessarily mean that the art of another tradition will make much sense. I think it fair to say that, in general, Catholic painting and sculpture tend to emphasize the more down-to-earth and familiar aspects of divinity and holiness. However otherworldly images of saints may be—wrapped in haloes, set against golden firmaments, performing marvels, undergoing unimaginable torment—they are almost always recognizably human. Images of a crucified God, writhing in agony, are a curious exception in that most of us are so familiar with them that we seldom find them shocking.

Hindu art, on the other hand, tends to emphasize the otherness and transcendence of the holy. Egyptian art of Pharaonic times offers a helpful parallel. Human bodies frequently have animal heads—Horus the falcon, Anubis the jackal, Sebek the crocodile, with the animal symbolism underscoring some particular aspect of the deity's special power and jurisdiction. But Egyptian art even at its most startling seems rather tame when compared to Hindu imagery. In addition to the use of an animal head on a human body, as in the case of Ganesha, Hindu iconography includes the use of multiple heads and limbs. The effect is even more arresting than the sight of a zoomorphic appendage, because although the multiple features are still apparently *human,* they represent a distortion that seems frightening to many viewers. A number of other features, such as facial expression, posture, gesture, or special symbol, can heighten that effect still further.

Monumental ferocity, wrath, and power communicate a sense of divine otherness, but Hindus generally take such imagery as a reminder that only scoffers need live in terror of divine vengeance. Some Hindu images underscore a deity's transcendence of the human by emphasizing physical attributes associated with attractiveness and canons of the supreme beauty. Idealized bodily proportions in both male and female form suggest at a glance that though the form may be recognizably human, the level of perfection is clearly divine.

Hindu iconography is complex and sophisticated, and a full interpretation of any given work of painting or sculpture will depend to a great extent on some awareness of the image's mythological references. But for starters it will help to keep a few general features in mind when you walk into the Asian galleries of your local museum. Multiple heads and limbs represent attributes or aspects of the deity's power. Each hand either grasps a special implement, such as a musical instrument or weapon, or makes an important gesture indicating protection for the devout or danger for the heedless. Posture is also very communicative; rigid frontality suggests aloofness, while the lithe "triple bend," the s-curve that appears when a standing figure shifts weight to one foot and tilts the upper body slightly, suggests greater approachability. Additional human figures in a picture or statue often represent either the deity's male or female counterparts, family members, other regular companions, or subordinate attendants. Each major deity in a visual presentation will usually be accompanied by some sort of animal "vehicle." Finally, it is important to keep in mind that while Hindus may revere a statue as a place on earth where God may choose to abide for a while, they do not worship the idol as such. Religious art merely points the believer toward realities infinitely beyond imagining.

59. I have heard that icon painters in the various Orthodox churches go through spiritual preparation as well as extensive training in traditional arts. Are there any parallels in Hinduism?

Ancient Christian manuals that prescribe fasting and prayer for artists, and give detailed descriptions of how to depict Jesus and the apostles, for example, have their Hindu counterparts. Traditional religious art has almost universally presupposed both that the artist is less an individual creator than a representative of the community, and that an effective work needs a spiritual foundation. Hindu manuals describing the proper way to execute sacred sculpture and architecture date back about two thousand years. The canonical principles originally applied to architecture were eventually extended to apply to sculpture and, to a lesser degree to painting, as well.

In addition to the various unique iconographic details that are associated with each name-form of the deity, a sculptor needs to consider first which of five "moods" or objectives the work is meant to communicate. The "peaceful" mode will have the subject in a posture of calm repose; the "perfect" mode will depict a firmly grounded figure; a sculpture in the "joyful" mode has weight shifted to one foot; the "wealth granting" and "wondrous" modes have corresponding postures. Special proportions must characterize each segment of a carved body, beginning with the feet, and including the legs and hips, the torso, arms, head, and face. Ideal figures are measured in multiples of the tala, or face length, with a set number assigned to every category of being, from trolls on up to the highest gods. Further specific proportional calculations determine how the sculptor will size the various body parts of each class of being. Even the spiritual energy of each subject to be depicted could be reduced to a set of mathematical proportions associated with an esoteric set of seven factors: excess, loss, bear or monkey, womb, water or treasure, lunar day, and fragment.

Many people in Hindu cultures still make their living as sculptors and painters of religious subjects, and the tradition of preparing spiritually for the work as for an act of devotion and merit remains alive, even if perhaps in somewhat diluted form.

60. What sorts of religiously important architectural forms have Hindus developed?

During the Vedic period, priestly officiants performed major religious rituals on open-air altars, in touch with the elements. Architecture was unnecessary for ritual, since the gods clearly needed no shelter and lived in their own greater or lesser cosmic spheres of influence. The Upanishads developed the concept of interior or spiritual sacrifice, but also laid the groundwork for the eventual development of more personal

imagery of the deity that would blossom into the various *bhakti* movements. Personal devotion in turn led to the growth of iconography along
with developments in narrative theology: if human beings are to cultivate relationships with their chosen deities, the gods will need a place to
reside among their devotees. Thus, to oversimplify a great deal, began
both sacred sculpture and religious architecture.

The earliest Hindu temples included two principal features. First
and most important was the "womb chamber" *(garbhagriha)* or inner
sanctum. Usually windowless and dark, with only one entry and room
inside for only an image and a few people, the womb chamber was the
house in which the deity could entertain select guests. Oriented along
the east-west axis, with the doorway facing east, the womb chamber was
often set toward the back of a rectangular plan, surrounded by a covered
ambulatory that allowed worshippers to circumambulate the chamber
before or after making their ritual offerings. The offerings themselves
were made on their behalf by the priest, who alone would enter the holy
of holies. Eventually elegantly sculpted stone temples grew in both size
and complexity.

Expanding the simple primitive ground plan, further antechambers
extended the eastward axis, creating a series of spaces dedicated to various ritual activities, including dancing and eating, through which worshippers made their way to the womb chamber. Meanwhile the elevation
also increased, with designers adding lofty spires called "mountain
peaks" *(shikhara)* over the womb chamber, and with the vaulting of the
antechambers descending in height toward the east. The resulting elevation recalled the mountain ranges wherein the gods dwelt on high even as
the womb chamber looked and felt like the inviolate cave of the heart in
which the deity was pleased to be confined for the sake of the devout.

Traditional requirements for the temple are just as stringent and
detailed as for religious sculpture. Ancient texts prescribe everything
from the choice of a religiously appropriate site, to laying out the ground
plan according to the symbolic geometric diagram called the *mandala,*
to ceremonies for dedicating the completed structure. One of the common Sanskrit terms for temple, *vimana,* means "well proportioned"; and
builders take special care to see that every feature of the structure con-
forms to the sacred mathematics that will make the temple perfect in its
correspondences to the divine realm. These documents are not merely
museum pieces. A few miles from my house, in St. Louis, the local

Hindu community has renovated its temple. An architect and his specially trained crew of *shilpis* came all the way from southern India specifically for the project of raising all the vimanas of five womb chambers through the roof of the simple original structure and adding a monumental facade tower called the *raja gopuram,* all according to centuries-old architectural and ritual practices.

Since cremation is the preferred funerary practice in Hinduism, the tradition has developed no monumental memorial architecture. And in spite of an ancient tradition of monasticism, there have been no major architectural developments explicitly associated with it. The temple is therefore the one major Hindu religious architectural type, but its history as an art form has been most remarkable, especially from the eighth through the sixteenth centuries. Carved from mountains of stone, the greatest of the temples are enormous sculptures dedicated to the holiness enshrined in the eternally fecund womb.

61. Is music as much a part of religious life for Hindus as it is for many Christians?

Like so many other aspects of Indian culture, Hinduism's musical heritage is so ancient that its origins are lost in myth. Indra is said to have had the original ensemble in his paradise. Krishna entrances all of creation with his flute. Hinduism's earliest scriptures were the Vedic hymns, always performed in a kind of chant still kept alive by a dwindling number of ritual specialists. Tradition attributes the earliest instrumental innovations to the sages *(rishis).* Narada, leader of a band of celestial musicians called Gandharvas, invented the classical instrument called the *vina,* now associated in iconography with Sarasvati, goddess of culture. Indians of a variety of religious communities have developed and used aspects of the national musical heritage, but Hindus have their own distinctive approaches.

Music's importance in Hinduism derives from the primal efficacious power of sound. A system of principal musical modes called *ragas* ("tints") acknowledges the power of music to move listeners and transform them spiritually. Each raga has its "female" counterpart *(ragini)* and its "sons" *(putra),* each of which is associated with a season and time of day and colors the spirit by establishing a mood. Major types of ragas with explicitly Hindu religious associations include, for example: a late-summer dawn raga called *Bhairava* ("terrible"), meant to instill awe and even terror in the presence of Shiva the ascetic; a south Indian raga called *Natanarayana* (Dancing Vishnu) fosters devotion for Vaishnavites; and numerous ragas have been associated with the romances of Radha and Krishna.

Virtually every major religious activity has its distinctive musical accompaniment. For example, when temple staff take the statue of the deity out for a "walk," musicians precede the group, preparing the way with auspicious sounds. Instruments fall into five categories depending on how they produce their sound. Ancient practice dictates the use of particular instruments for each deity's cult. Perhaps the best known Indian instruments, popularized outside of India since the sixties and seventies by virtuoso musicians like Ravi Shankar and Ali Akbar Khan, are the *sitar* and *sarod,* with plucked strings that produce a vast range of tonalities, and the droning *tambura,* said to have been a specialty of the sage Narada.

62. Do literary drama and theatrical performances figure prominently as religious art in the history of Hinduism?

Beginning with the stylized rituals of Vedic times, drama has been an important ingredient in Hindu life. On the steps of the great medieval stone temples throughout India, works of religious theater have been a classic type of performance art. It is not surprising that Krishna and Rama are far and away the most loved subjects, for they are major players in epic sagas. An ancient sage named Bharata is believed to have written a treatise on the dramatic arts, the *Natya-shastra.* Sanskrit dramatic works from as early as the fourth century remain popular. Bhasa (fl. 350) dedicated his finest play to Krishna's struggles with and eventual conquest of the evil King Kamsa. In addition to a large-scale play on a theme from the *Mahabharata* epic, the mysterious Kalidasa (scholars date him anywhere from 150 to 550) penned a drama about Rama that some think was his best work. More famous is his *Kumara-sambhava* ("The Coming to be of Kumara"), about Shiva's son Skanda/Karttikeya and his victory over the demon Taraka. The playwright's name, which means "Servant of (Shiva's consort) Kali" offers a hint as to why this last theme was appealing to him.

If Kalidasa was the greatest Sanskrit dramatist, many scholars believe Bhavabhuti (fl. 730) brought down the curtain on the art's golden age. He wrote at least two plays featuring the life story of

Vishnu's avatar Rama. A number of other plays on Vaishnava themes are extant from the next three centuries or so, but one stands out. Bengali poet Jayadeva (c. 1100) composed one of India's most popular Sanskrit devotional poems, the *Gita Govinda,* "Song of the Cowherd," as well as some Hindi hymns to Krishna. Still often performed in dance, the *Gita Govinda* develops the theme of Krishna's romance with Radha, his favorite among the *gopis* (milkmaids), using vividly amorous and sexual imagery that Hindu interpreters have understood as metaphors for the intense relationship between devotee and God. Radha must deal with intense feelings of jealousy as Krishna keeps her waiting or when she watches him dallying with others. At length they meet in the bridal chamber amid imagery reminiscent of the Song of Songs. When the story is acted out, male actor/dancers perform all the roles. Scenes from Jayadeva's work have also been a very popular subject for manuscript illustration.

63. A local Indian dance troupe occasionally gives public performances. Is there anything really "Hindu" about the ways Indians use traditional dance forms?

As in so many cultural and religious traditions, Hindu dance originated historically in liturgical ritual. Myth traces the origins of animated male dancing to Shiva's victory dance over a demon at Chidambaram in southern India, and graceful feminine dance to his wife Parvati, who first danced the "lively" *lasya* step. A type of classical temple dance called the *Bharata-natyam* was once the province of temple prostitutes but is still sometimes performed in the dance pavilions of major temples by a single dancer, who mimes texts like Kalidasa's romantic *Gita Govinda.* Because of its historic association with temple prostitutes, many Hindus look disapprovingly on sacred dance, but some dance companies remain dedicated to saving the art from oblivion. A very important and popular form of dramatic dance is called *katha-kali* ("story-play"). Beginning about the sixteenth century, the form developed under royal patronage. Typically performed only by male dancers, the highly energetic style features elaborate mime, accompanied by instrumental ensembles of percussion and strings, mostly on themes from the epics and puranas.

Much of the classical repertoire includes the same sort of complex iconography of gesture and posture that one finds in sculpture, with extensive enumeration of movements and positions for virtually every part of the human anatomy. It is an extraordinarily detailed stylized language of motion and pose. In fact, a series of sculptures on the temple to Shiva the Dance King in Chidambaram depict all 108 (that symbolic lunar number especially associated with Shiva) sequences. Choreography built on religious narratives typically puts together selected sequences that mime actions like milking a cow, for example, to tell a story like that of Krishna and the gopis. Folk dance forms also act out the romance of Radha and Krishna and Rama's conquest of Ravana, the demon who abducted his wife, Sita.

64. Given the antiquity of Hindu culture, one would expect Hindus to have a long tradition of hagiography and historiography. Is that the case?

Through much of the history of Hinduism, mythological stories have functioned somewhat as hagiography and historiography have in the history of Christianity, for example, or Islam. True Hindu hagiography or historiography did not develop until relatively recent times. It seems a surprising lacuna in the documentary legacy of so rich a cultural tradition, but perhaps not so odd when one considers that the category of mythic narrative is virtually missing from the sprawling written records of both Christianity and Islam. An eleventh-century Muslim scholar named al-Biruni observed after his travels in India that the Hindus simply did not care about chronology and were unable to identify significant events or movements in their history. It appears at first that we are dealing here with two very different views of human events and the passage of time. Perhaps so, but it is not helpful simply to pronounce the more historically precise "western" approach superior, as some scholars are inclined to do, declaring that Indian history would still be lost but for the work of Europeans. One simply has to look a bit harder at the sources for elements of an interest in history that is perhaps less well developed than in other cultural traditions, but significant nonetheless.

Biruni was not entirely correct in his criticism, for there are numerous important documents that do demonstrate a strong sense of passing events. India's two most famous epics, *Mahabharata* and *Ramayana,* revolve around divine heroes, and such historical elements as one finds are largely overwhelmed by their mythic surroundings; but the narrative framework is strong. The noted grammarian Panini (c. 300 B.C.E.), however, singles out a popular genre called the *akhyana* as a kind of historical, rather than explicitly fictional, story, suggesting an identifiable interest in early epic times in distinguishing myth from history. A number of other important but smaller epics, called *kavyas*, written between the fifth and fifteenth centuries exhibit a similarly mythic quality with their godlike protagonists. But biographies of notable historical figures began to appear in a form called *charita* from about the fourth century. Such works appear in greater numbers from late medieval times after the advent of Islam, with greater development in early modern centuries in the form of sectarian hagiographies of pivotal figures such as Chaitanya (1486–1533).

Seven:

Relationships to Other Religious Traditions

65. What is Jainism and what is its connection to Hinduism?

Jainism is one of the more important religious systems that came to prominence during the Upanishadic reassessment of Vedic ritualism. Jains (followers of the *jina,* "conqueror") trace their origins to pre-Aryan times, but the first significant historical evidence appears around the sixth century B.C.E. From the Hindu perspective, Jainism belongs to the category of splinter groups called *nastikas* ("nay-sayers," "deniers") roughly analogous to what Christians have called heretics. The Jain concept of time refines Hindu cyclicism by removing the need for divine intervention in ending and reinitiating cycles. Continuous natural movements of upward progress and downward entropy based on the eternity of matter constitute endless cycles. During each cycle a series of twenty-four "ford-finders" *(tirthankaras)* appear on earth to guide humanity.

A contemporary of the Buddha called Vardhamana Mahavira ("great hero," d. 476 B.C.E.) was the last tirthankara of the present cycle. Jains consider Mahavira a reformer rather than a founder. According to tradition, he grew up in the Bihari city of Vaishali, which would later be an important Buddhist center, and became a monk after his parents died. Mahavira inherited and developed the non-theistic view that liberation was entirely a matter of self-reliance and discipline. All things consist of *jivas* (living souls) encrusted in varying degrees with elemental materials called *ajiva* (the opposite of *jiva*). When a person chooses good and thus produces positive karma, its jiva is cleansed to some degree of ajiva and moves toward a more spiritual mode. The ultimate goal is to be entirely free of ajiva through a life of increasingly positive karma. Asceticism and noninjury *(ahimsa)* are the means, and early Jain tradition recommends stringent forms of both.

Jainism developed its own scriptures called *Angas* and *Upangas.* The former consist of eleven (some say up to fifty) loosely organized anthologies of various religious literary genres, from poems to sermons to canons of monastic discipline. There are described the "Five Great Vows" (reformer Mahavira added the fifth) that forbid injury to any living thing, lying, theft, sexual activity, attachment to wealth; and seven subordinate vows that govern actions such as travel and eating. The *Upangas* function rather as commentary, explaining the intricacies of proper karma. Some early Jains expressed their asceticism through the practice of nudism, but at an early council (c. 280 B.C.E.) convened for the purpose of editing the scriptures, a rift developed between the "sky-clad" and "white-clad" Jains. Claiming the authority of the twenty-third tirthankara, only the "white-clad" allow full monastic membership to women; the "sky-clad" forbid female monastic membership entirely and do not accept the scriptural canon.

Among the two to three million Jains now living in various parts of India, small numbers of monks maintain traditional types of austerity *(tapas)* and exercise extreme caution in all their actions to avoid injury to even the smallest living thing. Monks and nuns vow celibacy. Jain laity also vow truthfulness and marital fidelity, and engage in various forms of spiritual discipline. Since concern over noninjury closed certain occupations to Jains, many are now in professions such as law and finance and are among India's higher income groups.

66. What are the main features of Hinduism's relationship to Buddhism?

Siddhartha Gautama (563–483 B.C.E.), better known as the Buddha Shakyamuni ("Sage of the Shakya tribe"), was born and reared a Hindu. According to tradition his family was wealthy and belonged to the noble Kshatriya class. When Siddhartha was a baby, the story goes, his father consulted religious specialists for an interpretation of the child's unusual features. When they informed him that the boy was destined to become either a world-renouncer or a "wheel turner" (*chakravartin,* an ancient Indian expression for "mover and shaker"), the father determined that it would be the latter. But as Siddhartha became aware of the realities of sickness, death, and old age, he questioned the status quo and left home in search of his own truth.

He did not reject his Hindu heritage out of hand, but his understanding of that heritage was undergoing dramatic change. His spiritual odyssey took him to a series of teachers, two of them like the sages of the Upanishads, and through experiments in severe asceticism with as many as five Jain teachers. Still unsatisfied, Siddhartha sought a "middle path" between the extremes of hedonism and austerity, a path marked by evolving spiritual reinterpretations of the ancient concepts of karma, dharma, samsara, and moksha. Insight into the nature of human suffering and impermanence shaped Buddha's thinking. Like Jainism, early Buddhism replaced ritual propitiation of the gods with a demanding sense of individual responsibility. Buddha did not deny the existence of the gods, but did deny them any soteriological significance. Buddhist teaching replaced traditional understandings of dharma, especially as the foundation of social stratification, with a more personal code called the Eightfold Path.

But perhaps the most striking Buddhist turn of thought is its rejection of Hinduism's substantialist view that the core of every person is an indestructible soul that must either be set free or condemned to suffer the consequences of negative karma in subsequent rebirths. Buddha considered the notion of an immortal self that needs to be saved just one more delusion to grasp at in desperation, one more cause of suffering. Only the radical freedom of letting go even of the idea of a substantial self could break the cycle of craving. He did not deny the reality of rebirth for those who die still trapped in that cycle, but had to explain how a being without a substantial identity could be reborn. What or who is it that comes back around? It is the diehard *conviction* or consciousness that "I" am a discrete self that in effect constitutes the "something" that will endure another round of birth—such is the power of the illusion of selfhood. Finally, Buddha recast the idea of liberation (moksha), for there is nothing and no one to be liberated, into that of *nirvana* ("no wind"): by removing the fuel and air of craving, one extinguishes the fires of illusory selfhood.

Buddhism's relationship to Hinduism is like that of Christianity to Judaism to the extent that both later traditions rejected or dramatically reinterpreted central teachings of the parent traditions. Unlike Christianity, however, Buddhism rejected the authority of Hinduism's sacred scriptures as well.

67. What is Hinduism's relationship to Sikhism?

Muslim presence in India began around the eighth century and Islamic influence grew dramatically under a series of Sultanates during the thirteenth and fourteenth centuries. Intermittent violent conflict between Hindu and Muslim communities, especially in northern India, caused untold difficulties for both sides. A particularly tragic period began when Babur, founder of what would become the Mughal Muslim dynasty, led a military campaign against Delhi. In the latter fourteenth century a Punjabi Hindu of the kshatriya caste named Nanak (1469–1539), who experienced the resulting communal strife firsthand, decided to move toward a religious reconciliation. Growing up near Lahore in present day Pakistan, Nanak received traditional Hindu training, but also attended a Muslim school where he learned Persian, the language of the Muslim court.

Nanak began cultivating friends of both faiths and was especially influenced by a Hindu devotional movement centered around a group of mystical poets called the Sants, among whom Kabir (1440–1518) was a major figure. Kabir sang of the brotherhood of humanity, transcending both Hindu and Muslim scriptural authority, under a single divine guru. Nanak composed his own vernacular hymns developing Sant themes of social and religious equality, and taught the importance of the practice of communal singing *(kirtana)* so central to Hindu devotional life. Nanak's theology, like that of the Sants, was decidedly monotheistic. God communicates to humankind through gurus, designated as spokesmen and teachers, to their disciples *(sikhs)*. Toward the end of his life Nanak appointed his own successor. Sikh tradition would designate Nanak as the first of ten gurus, the last of whom, Guru Gobind Singh, died in 1708 after declaring that the scriptures would thereafter replace the living guru as Sikhism's central authority.

Nanak's hymns, along with some of Kabir's songs, are preserved in the Sikh scripture, the *Adi Granth* (Primal Book) or *Guru Granth Sahib*. A secondary scripture is the *Dasam Granth* (Book of the Tenth [Guru]), compiled by Gobind Singh and containing much Puranic material on Krishna and Rama. The scripture sits at the center of each Sikh place of worship, called a *gurudvara* or "abode of the guru." In a variation on the Hindu practice of temple puja, devotees awaken the scripture daily and put it back to sleep, just as Hindu temple officiants do for the image of the deity. Regular rituals involve hymns and readings from the scripture, performed by both women and men.

The tenth guru had also established the beginnings of a Sikh military wing called the *Khalsa* to defend against the Muslim Mughal dynasty. By the late seventeenth century this faith community, which had arisen out of a desire for interreligious understanding had grown into a military force engaged in battle against both Hindu and Muslim political powers. Britain defeated the Khalsa in 1849 and incorporated it into its law enforcement system. When the British partitioned India in 1947, the largely Sikh population living in the Punjab went through great turmoil as they watched the line of partition drawn straight across their land. Today what was once a single region is now half Pakistani, half Indian, but most Pakistani Sikhs gradually moved to the Indian side. Some have supported movements for Sikh independence and called for Punjabi secession from India.

68. What did the Second Vatican Council say about non-Christian faiths generally and about Hinduism in particular?

In the document *Nostra Aetate*, Vatican II's "Declaration on the Relationship of the Church to Non-Christian Religions," the Council made several very important statements about the official Catholic position with respect to several major non-Christian traditions. First, it declared that the church rejects "nothing that is true and holy" in traditions such as Hinduism and Islam, leaving unexplored the question of how one determines just which teachings those might be. Second, the Council reinforced the notion that non-Christian traditions present the possibility of salvation insofar as they are vehicles of grace, and to the degree that they are authentic responses to God's specific communication to their adherents. Third, Catholics are not merely to sympathize and tolerate non-Christians but to seek a positive regard for what is truly wonderful in their heritages. Finally, wrote the Fathers, other traditions can teach Christians of the diverse ways in which God communicates with other people and the unique ways in which the Spirit enlightens them.

There is tremendous latitude in Vatican II's references to other traditions. How does this general openness apply to Hinduism? *Nostra Aetate* speaks explicitly of Hinduism in only two full sentences, but they are important ones. It notes approvingly Hinduism's contemplation of the "divine mystery" as expressed in its abundantly fruitful mythological literature and philosophical systems. Secondly, the document mentions Hinduism's search for release from the human condition through the three paths of ascetical action, meditation in search of knowledge, and *bhakti's* "trusting flight toward God." The Council thus offers important clues as to what Catholics can see as "true and holy" in Hinduism, most

importantly that it represents an advanced and refined quest for the ultimate realities.

69. What sorts of theological themes do scholars use to compare Hinduism and Christianity?

Various Christian concepts invite especially interesting "theological dialogue" with Hinduism. First, a caveat: though theological concepts from two traditions may be similar in *form*—God becomes human,
three deities in one, divine power available to humanity, for example—
they may *function* very differently in the theological schemes of the two
traditions. Even in comparisons between Hinduism and traditions such
as Buddhism and Jainism, which use many of the same technical terms,
one has to be cautious about presuming that the terms are theologically
equivalent. The difficulty is still more acute when one compares traditions that have few obvious conceptual affinities, such as Christianity
and Hinduism. Bearing that in mind, one can draw a number of instruc-
tive parallels.

Take the notion of revelation, for example. Both traditions teach
that truth becomes available to humanity as an eternal divine "word"
(formal similarity). But there are major differences as to how human
beings experience the word. Hindus "hear" and "remember" the eternal
speech without historical reference; Christians know the word primarily
as embodied in Jesus and written in scripture, both concrete historical
events. Hindu revelation does not break into the forward march of time
as Christian revelation does. Hindu revelation is not supernatural as
such, since human beings are essentially divine to begin with; Christian
revelation in Christ elevates humanity.

Is the Christian notion of salvation analogous to the Hindu idea of
liberation *(moksha)*? Both appear to offer solutions to a central human
dilemma (formal similarity), but since the two traditions define the
dilemma in very different terms, the solution also plays very different
roles. Both traditions do, however, have broadly similar ways of formu-
lating the question as to the role of human effort in salvation—a variation
on the theme of the classic "faith and works" debate. Hinduism's Way of
Knowledge emphasizes the focused discipline needed to attain awareness
of the unity of all things; since there is no "other" to intervene and save,
grace is decidedly secondary. In the Way of Devotion *(bhakti),* the grace

of a loving deity is all-important, the various ritual activities fading into relative unimportance. But even here, two different emphases gave rise to the "cat school," characterized by the belief that God takes the initiative as the mother cat does; and the "monkey school," which teaches greater need for human effort, even as the baby monkey has to climb aboard and hold tight if it wants a ride. A major difference in the means of salvation between Hindu bhakti and Christianity is that whereas Christ enters fully into the suffering human condition, Krishna (and other avatars as well) does not save by dying.

Hindus and Christians alike are heirs to great theistic traditions and thus have a great deal to share concerning their central beliefs. Hindu theology speaks of Brahma, Shiva, and Vishnu as the *trimurti,* or triple form, but is that analogous to the Christian Trinity? The trimurti is a manifestation of a single deity in three forms, each omnipotent but associated with a characteristic work (creating, destroying, re-creating/sustaining). Sometimes the three are called *Sat-Chit-Ananda* (Being, Awareness, Joy), thus suggesting something of the essential nature of the Godhead; but in general the trimurti represents the divine in relationship to the universe. In Christian theology, the Trinity is as much about the very life of God (immanent trinity) as about God's external relations (economic trinity).

Finally, Christians readily see in the Hindu avatars a parallel to the doctrine of Incarnation. On a relatively superficial level, both concepts describe the descent of the divine into the world of humanity. Hindu and Christian theologians have debated many of the same general types of questions, such as whether the humanity that the deity assumes is real or only apparent ("docetism"), but there are major differences. The various avatars of Vishnu occur for different reasons, mostly to prevent the dissolution of the cosmos. Two of the principal avatars, Rama and Krishna, are intended primarily to save humankind from immorality and to punish evildoers. But since humanity is already essentially divine, Rama and Krishna do not assume the human condition in order to divinize it, but to rescue it from the powers of evil.

70. Are there any points of similarity between portions of the Krishna story and the story of Jesus? What is one to make of that?

On hearing the story of Krishna's infancy, one is immediately struck by what seem to be intriguing parallels with aspects of the story of Jesus, as well as with those of other important religious figures. There once was an evil king of Mathura named Kamsa, who seized power by imprisoning his father and usurping the throne. As a result of his evil deeds, the gods asked Vishnu to appear on earth to restore justice. About that same time, Narada, one of Kamsa's sages, informed the king that the king's own sister Devaki would give birth to a child who would bring an end to his reign. Springing into action, Kamsa hatched a plot to defend himself, ordering that all of Devaki's offspring be killed at birth.

Six children in a row he murdered. Toward the end of Devaki's seventh pregnancy, Vishnu miraculously transferred the fair-skinned Balarama to another woman's womb. When Devaki's husband, Vasudeva, impregnated her for the eighth time, Vishnu plucked a black hair from his own divine body and sent it to Devaki's womb. The miraculous result would be the dark-skinned Krishna. This time the king would take no chances, so he imprisoned and shackled Devaki and her husband. But at midnight, when the child was born, Vishnu caused the chains to break and cast a stupor over the guards. Slipping away with the baby, Vasudeva hurried to the country and left Krishna with his new foster parents, Nanda and Yashoda. Hearing of the escape, Kamsa gave orders to slaughter all newborn children, but Krishna again escaped miraculously. After foiling numerous attempts to catch Krishna through his early years, Krishna would eventually return to dethrone the evil king.

Some scholars suggest that it was only under the influence of contacts with Christianity that Krishna developed from the noble youth of earlier epic and legend into a deity. Main elements of Krishna's infancy narrative apparently first appeared around two millennia ago in the *Harivamsha (Genealogy of the Lord)*. But one need not propose that sort of cross-traditional connection to explain the situation, even if one could prove from which direction the influence came. Similar tales of the miraculous births and imperiled infancies of important religious figures have occurred in a variety of cultures. One can draw at least two significant points from this. First, great stories of wonder and danger seem to help adherents of religious communities all over to communicate their central truths. And second, legends travel, and sooner or later a tale we were sure was uniquely our own will turn up half way across the world—but that works from more than one point of view.

71. How did things go for the Hindu populations under Muslim rule in India, particularly under the powerful Mughal dynasty during the sixteenth and seventeenth centuries?

By the year 1000, many areas of India had already known Muslim presence for several centuries, and there is evidence of intriguing cross-fertilization between the two traditions. There had also been terrible tension. These are two very different religious systems originating in very diverse cultural milieux. Hinduism is doctrinally quite expansive, drawing from a range of scriptural sources spread out over two millennia. Islam traces its origins to a single prophet and scripture, and has suffered relatively little internal variance in doctrinal expression. Islam has always had an energetic missionary thrust, whereas Hinduism has had a genius for virtually swallowing other traditions and religious developments whole. Neither would budge, at least not officially."

But every religious tradition has its "crumple zones"—areas of thought and practice and social organization that eventually allow of significant interaction with other ways of looking at life. The earliest generations of Muslim traders soon began to marry Hindu women and work for Hindu nobility, but things did not go so smoothly once Muslims began to impose political control over parts of the subcontinent in the early eighth century. It seems clear that most of the Muslim invaders were more interested in gaining land and wealth than in gaining converts, but that did not prevent deeds of intimidation and religious self-justification, such as the destruction of Hindu temples.

Between the tenth and fifteenth centuries there was a great deal of interaction between Hindus and Muslims under many different circumstances: intermarriage, Muslims living under Hindu kings, Hindus living under Muslim rule, Muslims and Hindus living together where government was neither particularly Hindu nor officially Muslim. On the whole, Muslim rulers maintained official neutrality with respect to conversion. Copying the standard Muslim practice of levying a poll-tax on non-Muslims, some Hindu kings instituted similar taxes on their non-Hindu subjects. Positive religious interaction occurred most of all, it appears, on the level of popular piety. Sufi preachers (Muslims of mystical bent) were happy to gather non-Muslim followers, largely drawn from among lower-caste people and outcastes who appreciated Islam's more egalitarian spirit. Some Muslims would visit Hindu teachers as well, and it was the spirit of bhakti mysticism that often attracted such interaction. Always, however, there was more than enough polemical venom from the tongues and pens of Hindu and Muslim officialdom alike.

After the Mughal dynasty established itself in Delhi in the early fifteen hundreds, the Hindus under Muslim rule experienced a variety of fortunes over the next century and a half. Akbar (r. 1556–1605), one of the greatest of the Mughals and certainly the most colorful, pursued an active policy of interreligious toleration. He sponsored debates among members of various traditions, with Christianity represented by Portuguese Jesuits; he repealed onerous taxes on non-Muslim subjects; he even built Hindu temples and sponsored Hindu festivals. Akbar's descendants grew less tolerant, and under his great grandson Awrangzib (r. 1658–1707), official policy had come full circle. Even so, Awrangzib promoted far more Hindus to high ranking military positions than Akbar ever had. The story of Muslim-Hindu relations is long and complex, and well worth a much fuller investigation than this space allows.

72. How has the very substantial Muslim minority in modern India experienced life in a society so predominantly Hindu?

Perhaps eighty percent of India's nearly 950 million people are Hindu; at ten to twelve percent of the total, India's Muslims constitute the world's largest Islamic minority population. When the British began to take control of the subcontinent in the mid-nineteenth century, the largest political blocs they had to neutralize were Muslim. As the British East India Company gave place to a full-scale colonial government apparatus, the British generally favored Hindu interests. In addition, most Hindus found it much easier to adapt to the secular style of the British than to the radically different religio-cultural system of Islam. While the Hindus adapted readily to the new English language system of education, Muslims were slow to accept it. Many Muslims gradually found themselves reduced to working for the Hindus who had become the agents of the British. The Muslims of Delhi paid dearly for their support of the Mutiny of 1857, adding the disintegration of a large urban aristocracy to the continuing collapse of larger social structures dating back hundreds of years.

For the next ninety years, tensions grew as Hindus and Muslims more and more went their separate ways, both communities developing their respective revivalist organizations. Ram Mohan Roy (1772–1833), often called the Father of Modern India, founded the Brahmo Samaj (Society of [Those who Believe in] Brahman) in the hope that it would gather all believers in one God, but it attracted only Hindus and eventually spawned numerous other, less liberal, Hindu reform groups. Finding the Brahmo Samaj's embrace of non-Indian values unacceptable, Swami Dayananda (1824–83) formed the more militant Arya Samaj (Aryan Society) in hopes of galvanizing Hindus into identifying with their glorious past. He spoke openly against Islam as well as Christianity and the Hindu devotionalism he sought to reform.

Both sides had their separatists as well as their proponents of coexistence, but the separatists would eventually win out. Toward the end of the nineteenth century, a number of Muslim politicians advanced the idea that Muslims and Hindus were actually two distinct nations. Meanwhile militant Hindu ultranationalist Bal Gangadhar Tilak (1856–1920, dubbed the Father of Indian Unrest) turned up the heat on the other side by using religious festivals to spread his political message and by interpreting the *Bhagavad Gita* as a rallying cry for Hindus to do battle in the interest of self-preservation. Tilak advocated driving all non-Hindus from India's soil.

During the first half of the twentieth century, three Hindu lawyers, all educated in England, were voices of interreligious and political moderation. Mohandas Karmachand Gandhi (1869–1948), Jawaharlal Nehru (1889–1964), and Vallabhai Patel (1875–1950) all worked toward reform in the Hindu community and peaceful resolution of major social and religious rifts. One can at least imagine that, as tragic as the aftermath of Britain's separation of Pakistan as a Muslim state was, it would have been far worse but for the efforts of these three Hindus.

73. Does mysticism offer any significant prospects for Hindu relations with other faith communities that also claim mystical traditions?

Many people are tempted to think of mysticism as the common ground on which members of all religious traditions can come together happily. Respected scholars of more than one generation have produced carefully researched studies comparing aspects of Hindu mysticism with proposed parallels in well-known mystics of Christianity, Islam, and Buddhism. The view that ultimately all religious differences somehow meld together in the fiery crucible of religious experience, and that all the world's mystics are really talking about the same thing, is, however, as misleading as it is seductive.

There are certainly points of contact and clear similarities in the ways mystics of various traditions talk about their peak experiences. One can confidently point to a general correspondence of features such as heightened affect, bewilderment, apparent loss of personal identity, encounter with the ultimate reality, and the conviction that all religious differences are meaningless. But it is equally important to observe that the way mystics talk about their experiences, the language and imagery they use, is an essential component. When Hindu mystics talk about becoming one with Krishna or Brahman, they are describing experiences that are simply different than those of Christian mystics lost in God or wedded to Christ, or of Muslims drowning in the ocean of divine mercy or walking with the spirit of Muhammad.

What is going on here? A Hindu or Muslim mystic might say that in a moment of ecstasy he or she saw clearly that God cares not a whit to what faith community one belongs. Any mystic with a sense of history might be inclined toward a very careful choice of words, for more than a few have incurred the wrath of their respective religious establishments for seeming to play fast and loose with issues of religious allegiance. It's the ecstasy talking. When mystics speak of the object of their experience in imagery clearly drawn from a particular tradition, they describe an experience that simply cannot be reduced or homogenized to terms amenable to adherents of any other tradition. Even when a Hindu mystic talks of oneness with an unnameable, indescribable "All," he or she is still talking about that "All" from an identifiably Hindu perspective. In other words, there is no such thing as pure experience, even among certified mystics. All experience is mediated through, organized by, and made intelligible via the categories of religious language and symbolism.

74. Has monasticism functioned as a bridge in interreligious relations between Hindus and members of other traditions, as it has between Christianity and Buddhism?

From the perspective of interreligious relations, monasticism and mysticism both seem natural points of convergence. In the case of mysticism, it is the apparently congruent nature of the higher levels of experience described by members of diverse communities of faith. As for monasticism, the temptation is to assume that apparent similarities in institutional practices or organizational structures means a greater likelihood of religious affinity. Aren't monks and nuns really pretty much the same everywhere, give or take a few cultural differences? No more than mystics, alas.

Recent times have seen various interreligious congresses of members of monastic communities from various traditions, including Hinduism. It is relatively easy for the participants to compare notes about matters of external discipline and even about methods of prayer and meditation. But at the end of the day, when discussion gets down to why people do what they do and how they tell whether they are making progress, the underlying gaps open up. It is certainly beneficial for members of different traditions to educate one another, but educated nonmonastic types are just as likely to find common ground as monks and nuns. A great deal more study needs to be done on the history of Hindu monasticism before one can even be confident about making general parallels among traditions, since there are so many different types and styles within Hinduism. Even members of different Hindu orders find sufficient difference among themselves as to make deep interchange elusive.

75. What are some of the main developments in Hindu-Christian dialogue to date?

Serious Hindu-Christian interaction began with the arrival of Christian missionaries in India in the late sixteenth century. Jesuit Roberto de Nobili (1606–56) became a scholar of Sanskrit and Tamil and immersed himself so profoundly in the Hindu culture of south India that many acclaimed him a Christian Brahmin. His work represents an early milestone in comparative theology, but his ultimate intent was still conversion rather than dialogue as such. Hindu reform movements during the nineteenth and early twentieth centuries responded variously to Christian proselytism. Some reformers railed against Christianity's intimate association with alien values and British colonial rule. Some aided the cause of dialogue indirectly by insisting on the need to teach Indian children English. Others went so far as to claim that Hinduism's ample embrace could include Christianity within it. Until the twentieth century, nearly all Hindu-Christian interaction occurred within India.

About a century ago influential Hindu scholars such as Vivekananda and Radhakrishnan began spreading the word of their tradition among Christians in Europe and the Americas. They emphasized how certain universalizing tendencies in Christian thought could build a bridge to similar aspects of Hindu thought, and of Vedanta in particular. But the drift of their teaching was that Christianity would play the disciple to Hinduism's *guru*. Discussion began to move toward true dialogue in the 1960s, with leading roles played by Indian Christian groups and non-Indian scholars of Hinduism doing research in India. Much debate centered on whether or not genuine dialogue necessarily rules out missionary activity. More recently, Hindu scholars have connected with Christian thought via the ancient scholastic method of dialectic common to both traditions in different forms. They argue the need to understand the position of one's interlocutor well enough to reformulate it in such a way that the other side can still see their own truth in it, thereby advancing the discussion. The most important results of dialogue have been an insistence on the need for tolerance of religious diversity, the increasing availability of reliable scholarly studies of points of convergence and divergence, and an awareness of the centrality of interreligious understanding in the quest for world peace.

EIGHT:

WOMEN AND FAMILY

76. What sort of female role models do Hindu women find in their tradition?

Female role models begin to appear with early developments in narrative theology represented by the epics and puranas. The traditional model most widely recommended to young women is Sita, wife of the avatar of Vishnu called Rama. Sita is the heroine of the epic *Ramayana,* but above all, she is a wife who lives for and through her husband almost totally. Because her husband is her prime means of salvation, she will follow him wherever he goes, including harsh, unfair exile. While Rama is off hunting, a demon carries Sita away to Lanka, setting the stage for Rama's protracted effort to rescue her and defeat the demon. Rama then renounces Sita for the defilement she has incurred even by her unwilling association with the demon. Rather than submit to this opprobrium, she throws herself on a funeral pyre, but since she is pure the fire does not harm her, and Rama takes her back. In an episode added later, Rama again questions her virtue, exiles her, and expects another proof. Sita refuses, asks the earth to swallow her, and vanishes. Many women, especially outside traditional villages, no longer accept Sita as a model.

Another female image especially important among Vaishnava Hindus is Radha. Krishna (keep in mind that the myth is speaking about God here) the beguiling young cowherd, cavorts in Vrindavan, enchanting all with his flute. He lures the milkmaids *(gopis)* away from their husbands and plays hide and seek with them. Radha is Krishna's favorite gopi, although she feels jealous when he bestows his attention on the others. Krishna for his part also pines for her when they are apart. Radha is not Krishna's wife, but she steals away in the dead of night to be with him. This is by no means a story about marital infidelity; it is about a jealous God's total possessiveness of his lovers. Radha is willing to risk not only the dangers of the dark forest, but even loss of her reputation, to be with the Beloved. Her maid often acts as a go-between to set up their trysts. She will do anything for this relationship that offers neither wealth nor power, but promises the pinnacle of yearning love; and she knows that if for an instant she allows herself to grow possessive of Krishna, she will lose him. Unlike Sita, Radha embodies a symbolic type of the devotee who knows what an intimate relationship with God costs.

A third kind of role model is that of the powerful and immensely resourceful consort of Shiva named Durga ("inaccessible"). When all the male deities failed at the task of ridding the world of a troublesome buffalo demon magically invulnerable to either man or beast, Durga rose to the occasion—she was a woman and divine. Her most common early iconographic presentations show her defeating the beast; later her icons depict her astride her lion vehicle granting gifts to her devotees. Unlike any other female deity, she possesses the symbolic accoutrements of Vishnu: the discus, lotus, and club, as well as Shiva's sword and trident. She thus stands as the most prominent female symbol of total divinity and power. Durga also has her more domestic side, under the name Uma, as Shiva's consort. The combination of modes makes Durga one of the rare feminine name-forms of the deity who is capable of immense violence when necessary without becoming permanently horrific in appearance. Durga embodies the feminine divine energy called *shakti*.

77. What other Hindu goddesses are especially prominent in myth and legend?

Most Hindus acknowledge the feminine aspect of divinity under the generic names Devi ("the goddess," the feminine form of *deva*), or "the mother" *(ma),* or *shakti* (the feminine aspect of "power"). Worshippers frequently specify further by identifying their own chosen deity with any of several other name-forms. Some, such as Parvati, Laskhmi, and Durga, are known over large areas of India; others, like Vindhyavasini, Sheranvali, and Saranyu, are of more local interest. A few, like Ganga (the Ganges), are personifications of specific natural symbols. Tradition has conferred divine status on even the motherland herself, as the goddess Bharat Mata, "Mother India." All the goddess name-forms are ultimately the result of Devi's willingness to let herself be known in manifold ways.

Goddesses manifest female divine presence and power both as supreme beings, independent of their male counterparts, and as consorts. Virtually all of the great goddess-consorts also have considerable followings as distinct manifestations of divinity. Two of the consorts who function more or less independently in art and devotional life are Shri, consort of Vishnu, and Uma, consort of Shiva. Their roles as objects of devotion are never entirely disconnected from those of their consorts, and that works the other way around as well. God is never simply either male or female.

Uma, known also as Parvati, is a favorite subject of classical Indian sculpture. Myth identifies her as a reincarnation of Shiva's previous wife Sati, who had thrown herself on the funeral pyre. Shri ("fortunate") is more important as an independent focus of devotion. She is also known as Lakshmi, who in turn is said to have been incarnated as a different consort for each of Vishnu's avatars. Shri herself also has other "personalities," but is chiefly associated with prosperity and liberation. She functions as a mother and therefore as a mediator between God's children and their father. Without her there would be no saving grace, and she manifests herself in those situations most conducive to bestowing grace. Some have called her the immanent pole of deity to Vishnu's transcendent pole.

A curious collection of female deities called the Seven Mothers exhibit a number of interesting features in that most are named according to the feminine forms of their male counterparts' names. They embody explicitly the female energy or *shakti* of the gods, each identified with her god iconographically by depiction of the god's vehicle beneath her. But when depicted together, they are dancing to Shiva's tune. Varahi is the female energy of Vishnu's boar avatar, Varaha, who dived to the center of primal chaos to rescue the earth goddess, Bhu; she is the only one with an animal head. Kaumari represents the female side of Kumara, an alternate name of Skanda; Indrani is the feminine of the Vedic Indra; and Vaishnavi of Vishnu. They are sometimes depicted separately, usually dancing.

Whatever name-form she assumes, Devi manifests divine power in three ways: she sows illusion and then redeems from illusion; she divinizes earthiness and material existence; and she suffuses all things with an energy that is not always soothing. Like her male counterpart, the goddess exemplifies much about the ambiguity of existence as her devotees experience it. In addition to the goddesses associated with male counterparts in the "Brahmanical system," there are countless local and regional goddesses not linked with males, such as Shitala, the smallpox deity, but it would take a much larger book than this to deal adequately with all of them.

**78. Several Hindu goddesses are, you suggest, particularly
formidable. Could you say more about the fearsome feminine side
of the deity?**

Kali ("dark") is a female name-form associated with Shiva and
surely the most famous of the terrifying goddesses. She does not appear
prior to the Upanishads, where she is called one of the seven tongues of
Agni. In the *Mahabharata* Kali makes a cameo appearance as one of the
"seven mothers" *(sapta matrikas).* She comes into her own in a section
of the tenth century *Markandeya Purana* called the *Devi Mahatmya*
("Glorification of the Goddess"), conquering the most powerful of
demonic forces. With her fierce, wild-eyed visage, tongue lolling out
between blood-dripping fangs, necklace of skulls, and skirt of severed
arms, Kali is the other aspect of the charming Parvati whom devotees
want on their side.

Kali epitomizes the uncontrollable feminine. In one version of the
Ramayana, Kali has a significant role. After the demon Ravana defeats
Rama's troops, Rama's otherwise demure wife brings forth from her
forehead a wild Kali. Going on a manic rampage against the enemy, she
stops short of total cosmic destruction when she trips over Shiva and recognizes her more passive half (all relating to a pun: *shava* means
"corpse"). Kali's story clearly identifies the female as the energy, the
divine spark at the heart of reality, which confers on creation the power
of transcendence. Some images of Kali depict her as physically attractive (except perhaps for a pair of very long canine teeth), seated in a
teaching posture and making gestures of peace and largesse. She is
never without her hardware, however, the curved blade a reminder that
devotees must allow her to sever all their earthly attachments.

Chamunda, also one of the "seven mothers," is a manifestation of
Durga or Kali whose name comes from her slaying of the demons
Chanda and Munda. She is usually depicted as emaciated and hollow-
eyed, her six flailing arms each wielding a special weapon. She destroys
not only evil, but everything that is; nothing lasts, and the devotee wor-
ships her in the knowledge that the divine mother's power encompasses
every facet of existence.

Bhagavati (a feminine title meaning something like "blessed lady")
is a benevolent form of Kali who prefers to manifest herself under the
wrathful feminine name-form Bhadrakali. An example of a more localized goddess, Bhadrakali is the chief deity of Kerala. This virgin-mother-

siren-warrior encompasses every aspect of reality from the loveliest to the most gruesome. Heat and flame are the special attributes of this red goddess, who is a veritable "ball of fire." Devotees frankly admit to worshipping her out of stark fear that if they slacken in their devotion they will pay a terrible price, yet part of her ritual has young men taunting her to stoke her fury.

Arresting images of this sort are among the ways people in traditional Indian societies have sought to deal with issues of gender and sexuality. The reservoir of such imagery is vast and deep, supported by an almost endless store of myth and legend that interprets so much of life in traditional cultures. These three examples are only the merest hint of an immensely more complex reality.

79. Are any women numbered among the great religious teachers and saints?

Women were among the authors of the earliest Vedic hymns, but after the Vedic period few women appeared in prominent religious positions for a very long time. In various sectarian movements, especially those that deliberately stepped outside the careful observance of caste and similar social strictures, women have occupied places of prominence. One of the Tamil Vaishnava Alvar poet-saints of the ninth century was a woman known as Andal. Legend has it that she remained unmarried out of devotion to God. Walking up the steps of the temple where she prayed incessantly, according to the lore, Andal embraced the deity's image and became one with it.

A number of women have been acclaimed as gurus in local or regional settings. Nirmalasundari Bhattacharya, for example, was born in Bengal in 1896. Given to ecstatic states as a child, she married at thirteen; but the marriage was never consummated and her husband became a sannyasin with his teenage wife as his guru. Her ecstatic behavior continued into her fifties but gradually mellowed into trance-like absorption. As an act of devotion, her followers, who considered her none other than Devi herself, used to gather to watch her. At the age of twenty-six, Nirmala began the structured discipline of sadhana without previous instruction, then initiated herself and assigned herself a mantra—all behavior unheard of among more orthodox gurus. After keeping a silent vigil for three years, she moved into a period of what she called effortless being, pure play, total spontaneity. Playing the holy fool, she mimicked the *lila* of the gods. Eventually she returned from the fringes of society to found an ashram, but Nirmala continued to engage in puzzling symbolic behavior. She would occasionally curl up into a fetal position inside the egg-shaped altar in the ashram, and was given the name Anandamayi Ma (Bliss-filled Mother). She continued her spiritual ministries in the ashram till she died in 1982.

Women saints continue to be important personalities all over the India, especially in rural villages. Often they "channel" the words of the gods as a service to other villagers. These are sometimes younger married mothers who make the case for their own sainthood, but more often they are older women first called saintly by others. In a way, villagers acknowledge their leaders by thinking of them and treating them as especially holy.

80. It sounds as if most Hindu rituals focus on and are performed by men. Are any rituals explicitly for, or administered by, women?

In Vedic times women took equal part in leading the majority of religious observances, and some fertility rituals only women could lead. But with the rise of the Brahmanical priesthood, women's roles in official religious practice dwindled dramatically. Female yogis and sadhus are not nearly as numerous as their male counterparts, though tradition explicitly sanctions those options. One of the important factors at work in many of these exceptions to the "official" mode, thereby perhaps making women's participation less threatening, is that yogis and sadhus have by definition stepped outside of the ordinary boundaries of both caste and gender distinctions. In some segments of Hindu society women function as *pandits,* specialists in religious ritual. But the only textually sanctioned religious activity traditionally allowed *only* to females is that of *devadasi* ("servant of God"), young women who are espoused to the deity of a particular temple but allowed to have human sex partners.

Women also participate as ritual leaders in many settings not "officially" sanctioned by the religious establishment, such as local annual festivities. Women in rural areas often band together in temples to conduct communal worship in song, offering their bhajans an hour or two before the men come to chant. Even when men in the countryside join the local women, the women often lead the prayers. Women preachers, of the Brahmin caste frequently, often make the rounds of rural temples. At these gatherings all are welcome regardless of caste or marital status. Some shamans are women, and the role of the Hindu midwife includes many elements of ritual through which they guide their clients. In short, women enjoy a good deal of religious authority and leadership at the popular level, but little or none of any hierarchical standing.

81. How would you characterize the status of women in Hindu tradition generally?

There is no doubt that Hindu tradition, beginning at least with the early legal treatises, has held womankind in tragically low regard. Not least among the disastrous results have been the overwhelming desire for male children, the practice of infanticide, and, more recently, the denial of medical care to endangered infant girls in favor of infant boys. Gender discrimination runs very deep in the tradition. The *Bhagavad Gita* and its literary matrix, the *Mahabharata,* generally relegate women to the spiritual ash heap along with outcastes and slaves. The *Laws of Manu* offers a detailed catalogue of female evils and divine sanctions designed to minimize the destruction that can emanate from all things womanly: since women are the cause of so much evil and contamination, one can kill them as one might kill an untouchable, with scarcely a second thought.

Women, according to this perspective, pose a nearly cosmic threat that only the strictest regulation can hope to contain. Myths of the more free-ranging goddesses ironically prove the point even as they offer virtually the only broad-based cultural affirmation of female strength and capability. Much of the mainstream myth tethers many of the exploits of the goddesses to the implicit or at least tacit approval of their consorts, but some of the sectarian literature as well as more local lore depicts the mythological equivalent of the truly "liberated" woman. In spite of the efforts of modern reformers who saw clearly that when women lose, the whole of society suffers, women's rights as Hindus remain truncated. For example, a widow does not have the right to total control over her inheritance, but must deal with her husband's male heirs, who stand to gain when she dies, regardless of her wishes.

Inequality in educational opportunities had been a major problem for women in Hindu societies for centuries and, as in many other cultural contexts, has begun to change for the better only in relatively recent times. Though some scholars believe that in the Vedic period girls and boys received largely the same education, by the end of the first millennium B.C.E., women were forbidden even from hearing, much less studying, the Vedas. Initiation into formal study was strictly limited to higher caste boys and, as a result, in India virtually no women have joined the ranks of Hinduism's scholars and teachers in the academic system as such.

82. Classical Hindu artists have often depicted the goddesses in a highly idealized, even dramatically exaggerated, form. What does that suggest about the place of real women in Hindu societies?

Representations of both masculine and feminine divinity in many cultures have tended toward the unrealistic or even bizarre. We are, after all, talking about how to give expression to what is by definition beyond expressing. Exaggeration of human features and qualities is a natural tendency, one that has often occurred throughout history when humans have depicted the divine in human form. Artists often begin with the fullest expression of any desired attribute and imagine what it would look like taken to the "nth" degree. The ancient Venus of Villendorf is an earthy icon of fertility and fecundity, the very essence of plump. Images of the Middle Eastern goddess Ishtar sometimes depict the earth mother with multiple breasts to suggest infinite nurturance.

Hindu art has its distinctive ways of suggesting feminine divine perfection in both attractive and fear-inspiring modes. Parvati, Uma, Lakshmi, and a host of other female deities appear especially in sculpture as models of feminine beauty and sexuality. Explicit canons of proportion and rules of iconography dictate that posture be usually languid and inviting, but rarely inelegant; that physique feature perfectly round full breasts, very narrow waist and rounded hips; and their accoutrements include the specific types of jewelry and symbols associated with each deity.

One need not assume any sort of blatant gender bias here, except in the canon that requires images of female deities to be about a third smaller than those of the male deities with whom they are designed to appear. A similar stylization is at work in the depiction of male figures. Suggesting the power and presence of Shiva by reducing the deity to his aniconic symbol, the *linga,* is an obvious example. In any case, the final conclusion of all Hindu theology is that even though human beings find it nearly impossible to conceive of an ungendered deity, God is infinitely beyond gender. Hindu God-talk acknowledges that truth very concretely, in that it almost always gets around to including both the masculine and feminine aspects of any given deity. If Shiva is here, so is Parvati, even in the aniconic combination of linga with female *yoni.*

One of the most intriguing genres of religious imagery is that of the androgynous or bisexual deity. Shiva is often depicted as *Ardhanarishvara* ("Half-woman Lord"), both in painting and in sculpture. From the tip of the headdress to the soles of the feet, the image is divided exactly down the middle, with Shiva's features on the image's right and Parvati's on the left. There are some examples of similar treatments of Vishnu, but relatively few. The underlying issue is the quest for a way to depict divine perfection and, therefore, otherness from the ordinary.

83. Christians are familiar with images of a "holy family," and I wonder if there is anything similar in Hinduism?

Shiva and his wife Parvati, along with their two offspring, Ganesha and Skanda, form a most interesting variation on the theme of the "holy family." The charming, well-bred Parvati turns out to represent the closest thing to normalcy in the set. She is loving and highly domestic, but because Shiva is gone so much of the time she becomes lonely and needs someone to protect her. Miraculously, Parvati creates a son from the dirt she rubs from her body while bathing one day, and stations him to guard the door. When Shiva comes home and sees the strange young man, he removes the intruder's head. The gods instruct the headless Ganesha to take the head of the first forest creature he finds facing north. He thus becomes the elephant-headed deity whose task is to oversee comings and goings.

The genesis of their second son, Skanda or Karttikeya, is an even more unusual combination of divine actors. The ancient Vedic gods Agni (fire) and Soma (the sacred juice) spy on Shiva and Parvati as they make love. When Shiva notices the voyeurs, he casts his scalding hot seed into Agni's mouth. In variants of the story, Agni then either spits the seed out, and it becomes a mountain, or he spits the seed into the Ganges, which then deposits it on the shore, where the Krittikas and Matrikas raise it to become Karttikeya/Skanda. Skanda therefore has multiple parentage, as symbolized by his six heads. As a child-god, Skanda was given to child-grabbing, a habit both fearful and fortunate, in that he symbolizes both danger to children and divine protection for them.

Artists have often depicted this holy family either descending together from their mountain abode of Kailasa or having a picnic of sorts, often in a cremation ground. Parvati rides her lion or serves Shiva his favorite beverage. A naked Shiva (sometimes shown with five heads), his hair matted with cremation dust and entwined with serpents, sits astride his bull Nandi or leans against a tree. Little six-headed Skanda enjoys riding on, or offering a snack to, his peacock, and handing his father another skull to thread onto his necklace. Ganesha rides his rat—a bit of humor, since elephants are said to be afraid of rodents, never mind the size disparity. Ganesha enjoys his sweets in the company of Nandi and the lion. Variations show Ganesha riding Nandi or carried by Parvati as she rides the bull.

Hindu sculptors have frequently portrayed somewhat more conventional images of the family in a grouping called "Somaskanda," an elision of the names of Shiva, his wife Uma (an alternate name of Parvati), and Skanda, who appears in these compositions as a normal if perfectly proportioned youngster. Occasionally mother and father appear only with Ganesha, and other bronzes often show the parents alone as a loving couple. There is no Vaishnavite counterpart to this family imagery, apart from the loving couple genre, since Vishnu and Lakshmi have no offspring as such. In Vaishnavite imagery the metaphor of the avatars communicates the deity's pervasive power and presence.

84. I've heard the practice of ritual suicide has not been uncommon among women in India. Could you explain?

The practice of female self-immolation is called *sati* (often anglicized as suttee) after Shiva's wife Sati, who killed herself when her own father insulted Shiva. The custom of widows throwing themselves on their husband's cremation pyre is certainly post-Vedic and is first attested during the epic period (400 B.C.E.–400 C.E.). (I mentioned earlier that Rama's wife Sita also attempted suicide, but for different reasons). Legal texts had begun to speak favorably of the practice nearly two millennia ago, and by the early middle ages it had become common for princes and warriors of the Kshatriya varna to burn not only with several wives, but with female blood-relatives and concubines, and female servants as well. The practice spread all over India and grew more frequent through the middle ages and into early modern times. When first the British arrived in India in the mid-eighteenth century, they preferred not to interfere in what appeared to be religious practice. After much lobbying, especially by Ram Mohan Roy, founder of the reformist Brahmo Samaj, the practice was officially outlawed in 1829. Reports of scattered incidents of sati have nevertheless continued until very recent times.

Many religious and social motives are listed among reasons for the practice. It seems clear that relatively few of the many women who have been burnt alive over the centuries freely chose to die that way. Tradition has variously described such motives for the practice as the certainty of instant salvation, an opportunity to preserve the honor of the family, fulfillment of the duty of every good wife never to leave her husband no matter what, and the desire to save oneself from the miserable fate of widowhood.

85. Are there distinctively Hindu views on marriage rituals and practices?

Most Hindus, whether in cities or villages in India or elsewhere, still prefer the traditional practice of arranged marriage, including 85 to 90 percent of India's marriages, of whatever religious tradition. In cities like New Delhi, elaborate processions wind through the streets as the groom heads for the wedding on his white horse. Even families of modest means will incur enormous debts to provide feasts and dowries for their daughters. Many families retain the services of marriage brokers, whose task is to seek out eligible prospective daughters-in-law who meet the qualifications set out by the parents of either bride or groom. Traditional marriage brokers are specialists in genealogy. Many families also refer to marriage ads that are a regular feature of newspapers.

Caste compatibility often remains more important than educational and financial parity, although concern for dowry is sometimes a critical factor. Dating, romantic love, and courtship are largely unacceptable in orthodox Hindu society. The period of communication and initial familiarity often includes exchange of horoscopes and photos. Relatives of the young man and woman may exchange visits to each other's homes; he may offer gifts to the future bride and there may be a discussion of dowry. Several chaperoned meetings offer opportunities for parties to become minimally acquainted and to opt out if they have serious reservations, although such meetings are a relatively recent variation on the traditional pattern. Ongoing communication usually occurs through parents or other go-betweens.

Marriage is one of the Hindu *samskaras* or rites of passage, and astrologers often choose the appropriate moment. Traditional weddings, at least in upper-caste families, include a "giving away" segment and the marriage rite itself. During the first part, guests arrive at the bride's home or perhaps at a hotel. Two Brahmin priests, one for each family, recite the genealogies. After the bride's father indicates his approval of the young man, he presents symbolic gifts to the bridegroom. Attendants bring the bride in and her father formally gives her away, pronouncing again the young couple's genealogies. Part two, called "taking the hand," includes a lengthy chanting of sacred texts by a priest while the couple sit cross-legged before a fire. At the conclusion of the ceremony the bride and groom circumambulate the fire clockwise, the bride indicating her consent by taking seven steps to ask for all the blessings of prosperity and progeny. It is common for the bride to make several extended visits to her parents' home during the first year.

Since there is a great deal of variation, these are only a suggestion as to some of the major features of traditional practice. Numerous local and regional customs attend the separate preparation for both bride and groom prior to the actual ceremony.

86. Does Hinduism permit divorce, remarriage, and polygamy? Is marriage practice more restrictive for women than for men? What about incest?

The Laws of Manu decreed that since marriage was eternal and indissoluble for women, they were traditionally unable to divorce or remarry if widowed. This stricture has never applied to men. Women have had no recourse in the event that a husband commits adultery. Reform efforts during the late nineteenth and early twentieth centuries have secured the right of remarriage for widows, and since 1955 the Hindu Marriage and Divorce Act has allowed them to divorce for cause as well, but the practice is still relatively rare. Women have been taught to put up with all difficulties, no matter what, because their husbands are their lords and masters. Even when under certain rarely applied legalities a woman might leave her husband because of terminal illness, impotence, or insanity, the woman could not hope to find another husband. Men have always had the right to dissolve a marriage for virtually any reason merely by shutting the wife out of the house. Newer legislation lists cruelty, apostasy, more than five years of insanity or desertion or certain diseases, impotence, or the husband's concubinage as valid causes for divorce, but only for marriages of less than twenty years' duration.

Polygamy and concubinage both have ancient roots in Indian culture, beginning with the Aryan invaders. In some areas, women have taken more than one husband, though in general polygyny (marriage to more than one wife) is the predominant form. Some forms of polygyny have allowed sexual relations across caste lines even when formal marriage across those lines was not countenanced. In modern times, similar practices continue on a much more limited scale in rural areas and are quite the exception; monogamous relationships are definitely the rule.

Women generally have been under much more rigorous judgment than men as to their eligibility for marriage. Although virtually any man who is not impotent, insane, or the victim of a terrible disease is considered marriageable, traditional norms make sweeping demands on women, beginning with the expectation that she has never been married before. Some families will still not allow a younger daughter to marry if an older daughter remains single. The medieval legal texts even stipulate general physical and emotional qualifications for a prospective bride. She should be, for example, practical in managing household matters, attractive, docile, and eager to produce children and give her husband pleasure.

Among certain ruling families through the ages, and in some rural areas, incest has been relatively common. According to some scholars there is even solid evidence for scriptural sanction in the Vedas—a feature rendering them by no means unique among religious texts over two to three thousand years old. But in modern times, incest generally carries a severe taboo among Hindu families.

87. Is there a significant "women's movement" among Hindus in India?

Late nineteenth-century reform movements such as Brahmo Samaj and Arya Samaj were the first modern attempts to address women's concerns in a systematic fashion, and dozens of large nationally based women's organizations emerged during the first half of this century. But the Independence Movement represented the greatest single advance of its kind in the twentieth century. In the fifty years since India's independence, women have made enormous strides toward social and religious equality. Many of the issues that fueled the movement for independence were in fact pressed by and on behalf of women. The Constitution clearly grants women equal rights, and in the late forties and early fifties various national legislative initiatives, some explicitly directed at the situation of Hindu women, addressed major problems in all facets of women's lives, from employment to dowry to divorce to property rights. Unfortunately, legislation has often simply not been enforced, and conditions for many women have changed little. Social structures and patterns many hundreds of years old are exceedingly difficult to modify.

Outsiders might think that a nation of nearly a billion people open enough to have a woman, Indira Gandhi, as its elected leader must have gotten its act together with respect to gender roles. But India is surely one of the world's most socially complex countries. Many women's organizations have continued the struggle, with increasing membership especially through the seventies and eighties. Middle class women have established resource centers and shelters serving anywhere from dozens to thousands of women a year in cities and towns all over India, but they come nowhere near to being able to fill the need.

Hindu women have been publishing serious critiques of India's dominant religious and social systems for decades, though few have referred to their work explicitly as feminist, even very recently. A number of formal programs in Women's Studies have developed in major universities in cities like Bombay and Delhi, to address matters of concern to women of all religious and social backgrounds. Even the more militant feminists in India tend to use much more indirect tactics than their counterparts in America, for example. They must contend with a system that remains dead set against extending to the millions of lower-caste women the kinds of freedoms high-caste women have managed to achieve since the late nineteenth century, often with the assistance of well-educated and relatively liberal minded husbands and fathers.

One thing seems clear, however: Hindu women, along with Indian women of other religious heritages, are contributing to a global social revolution that will ultimately succeed and in comparison with which every other social movement this century will seem inconsequential.

NINE:

HINDUISM HERE AND NOW

88. What is the significance of Mahatma Gandhi from a Hindu point of view?

Mohandas Karmachand Gandhi (1869–1948) was probably the most famous Hindu of the twentieth century, and for very good reason. Son of a man who had served three terms as a local prime minister, he grew up in a family for whom political involvement was a way of life. He was born into a Gujarati Brahmin caste that, partly as a result of some intermarriage with Shudras, became the ancestors of a Vaishya, or merchant, caste called the Modh Bania. His family were Vaishnavites especially devoted to Rama and Krishna. Denounced as an outcaste for choosing to go to England, Gandhi received a degree in law at the University of London. He returned to India for a few years and left again in 1894 to practice law in South Africa. There he experienced racial bigotry first hand and began to form his thought on how to fight the injustice it represented. In South Africa he founded the Natal Congress to secure rights for the Indians of that country. Gandhi returned to India in 1915 and spent the rest of his life dedicated to the struggle for Indian independence.

Gandhi had married at age thirteen, had four children, practiced lifelong vegetarianism in the interest of living more simply, and gave himself more and more to the austerity of the type of asceticism called *vairagya.* In his personal spirituality he blended the Sermon on the Mount and the *Bhagavad Gita,* both of which he discovered while in England. His experience of becoming an outcaste made him a special patron of the people he called "Children of God" *(harijan).* Oddly enough he did not denounce the caste system, but merely argued that all castes are equal and ought not keep people segregated. In his struggle for justice and for the dispossessed, he developed the ancient Hindu tradition of *ahimsa* into a means of political action expressed in passive resistance and in his own use of public fasting.

During the 1920s and 30s he led a series of social justice campaigns. He taught economic independence, called for cooperation between warring Hindus and Muslims, and decried society's treatment of the untouchables. Gandhi was against partitioning India, but massive riots persuaded India's politicians to accede to the demands of Muhammad Ali Jinnah (1876–1948), known as the Father of Pakistan. *Satyagraha* ("truth-grasping") was Gandhi's way of describing his whole life. His autobiography, *The Story of My Experiments with Truth,* is the chronicle of his search for a God who *is* Truth. A believer in the equality of religious paths, Gandhi taught total respect for the beliefs of others and deplored proselytizing.

He came to be known popularly as the Mahatma, Great-Souled One, an epithet he earned not least because of his belief that faith is a call to loving service based on the conviction that all life is one seamless reality. He taught his followers that nonviolent resistance was not a tool for punishing an enemy but for converting the other out of love. I believe his genius was his insight into the need for simplicity in one's choice of means for living, out of concern that there be enough for all. But his focus on the here and now never overshadowed his conviction that liberation remained the ultimate purpose of life. And the great irony of his life is that this man of peace fell to an assassin's bullet, that of a Hindu enraged that Gandhi was yielding too readily to Muslim demands. Gandhi died on January 30, 1948, as India was gaining its independence.

89. Have there been any other major Hindu religious leaders in modern times?

Several very important figures associated with modern Hindu revival movements, sometimes called neo-Hinduism, stand out. Ramakrishna Paramahamsa (1836–86), born Gadadhar Chatterjee, was a visionary of Bengal. His family were Vaishnavite Brahmins and he grew up active in temple life and ritual, succeeding his older brother as priest of a Kali temple just up river from Calcutta. For a time he studied Vaishnavite bhakti and Tantric rites, and Shankara's Vedanta *sadhana* (meditation), but remained a devotee of Kali. Experienced as he was in all of Hinduism's main spiritual methods, from karma to tantra, Ramakrishna's reputation for holiness rapidly elevated him to sainthood, a cause championed by his most famous and influential disciple, Vivekananda. He wrote nothing and argued that book knowledge was worthless insofar as it did not lead to the experience of God. He experimented with devotional aspects of both Islam and Christianity and decided that any religion could be a path to God.

Swami Vivekananda, originally known as Narendranath Datta (1863–1902), met Ramakrishna at the age of eighteen and became an ardent follower. Unlike his uneducated country teacher, however, Vivekananda was polished, cosmopolitan, and eloquent. He is perhaps best known abroad for his address at the first Parliament of World Religions in Chicago in 1893. To spread his teachings on neo-Vedanta, he formed the Ramakrishna Mission in 1897, connected with a religious order, and traveled extensively in Europe and the United States. A recent edition of selections from his eight volumes of letters, lectures, and essays called *Vedanta: Voice of Freedom,* offers an excellent survey of Vivekananda's thought. Some believe his work first made it possible for modern Hindus to understand their tradition as a unified whole offering a full range of spiritual possibilities, each tailored to specific needs and capabilities. Vivekananda envisioned Hinduism, the "mother of all religions," as the hope for a united world, and taught that Buddha and Christ were, along with Krishna and Ramakrishna, divine avatars.

Sarvepalli Radhakrishnan (1888–1975) became one of the chief exponents of neo-Hinduism's blend of Vedanta with themes of Protestant liberalism (as a way of countering Christian missionary activity) and European (especially neo-Hegelian) philosophy. Though he was born in a Telugu-speaking area of south India, he was much influenced by the Bengali Vivekananda. Some scholars criticize Radhakrishnan's interpretation of Indian religious philosophy as inaccurate and misleading because it is too contaminated with non-Hindu concepts. They argue that in his striving to revive a languishing tradition he ends up simply confusing the issue. Advocates of neo-Hinduism, however, highly regard Radhakrishnan's view that Hinduism is the closest thing available to a universally valid religious tradition.

90. Is there such a thing as "Hindu fundamentalism"? On the other side of the coin, are there many "secularized" Hindus nowadays?

"Fundamentalism," understood negatively as a kind of intolerant literalism or militant traditionalism, is part of the religious landscape virtually everywhere and in every age. Strangely enough, there is no entry in the *Encyclopedia of Religion* on the subject, and the only index entries connect the phenomenon solely to Christianity and Islam. There have been several important manifestations of fundamentalist thinking in the history of Hinduism. One is the organization called Arya Samaj, founded by Dayananda Sarasvati (1824–83), from the same region of Gujarat that was Gandhi's home. He began his public work in 1863 and formed the Samaj in 1875 as a reform movement. Its purpose was to reclaim the most ancient roots of Hinduism by purging it of centuries of scriptural and doctrinal contamination. In addition, the Arya Samaj sought to counter anti-Hindu Christian polemics, but its own counter-polemic was every bit as virulent in its condemnation of Islam and sectarian Hinduism as well as Christianity.

In its repudiation of all but the earliest scriptures, the Vedas, Arya Samaj recalls the Torah-only stance of the biblical Sadducees. Its rejection of all subsequent developments, such as the ways of knowledge and devotion, in the interest of recovering a pure Vedic monotheism is reminiscent of the Islamic Wahhabi movement's plan to purify Islam of all belief deemed non-Qur'anic. Unlike some other militantly traditionalistic movements, however, the Arya Samaj promoted equal participation in ritual and scripture study by women, outcastes, and other marginalized members of Hindu society. Unfortunately, its religious and intellectual exclusivity prevented its program of social openness from attracting large numbers. Additional elements from Arya Samaj's ten "fundamentals" include belief in one true perfect God, strict personal and social ethics emphasizing common good over individual desire, and rooting out ignorance through scientific investigation.

More recently a number of political parties built on largely religious platforms have been making their presence felt in India. The Bharatiya Janat Party (or BJP), perhaps the most influential of these religio-political factions, has been gaining seats in various state legislative bodies for some years, but its prominence increased dramatically in the early 1990s. The BJP lent its support to the militant Vishva Hindu Parishad organization's call for the destruction of a sixteenth-century mosque in Ayodhya, claiming that it stood on the site of the birthplace of the god Rama. Riots ensued and the mosque was virtually leveled in December 1992, but the Supreme Court refused to rule on whether the Hindu factions could proceed with their plans to build a temple to Rama there.

Secularism, which some devout Hindus attribute to the "western" influence that rode colonialism's coattails into south Asia, has naturally had a profound impact on many Indians whose family roots go deep in Hindu tradition. Some college-educated city dwellers regard ancient devotional practice as so much hocus-pocus and dismiss the historical dominance of the Brahmanical priesthood over the pious masses as institutionalized superstition and social manipulation. Others regard even the more moderate among the various reform movements as grasping at straws, a vain attempt to snatch a meager fistful of tradition from the jaws of modernity. Even so, many thoroughly secularized Indians still identify themselves as "Hindu," either because they see a historic inseparability between Hinduism and Indian ancestry or to distinguish themselves from Indian Muslims, Christians, Sikhs, and Jains. There are, in other words, some people for whom a cultural Hinduism functions as a reflexive identity, just as there are countless doctrinally and ritually marginal Christians and Muslims who call themselves Christian and Muslim as if by default.

91. Has there ever been a Hindu "Reformation"?

Some scholars liken the movements spawned during the nineteenth century to Christianity's Reformation period. Brahmo Samaj (Society of God), founded in 1828 by Ram Mohan Roy (1772–1833) of Bengal, was one of the first and most durable of several major reform movements. A signal event in his efforts for reform was Roy's vigorous support of legislation forbidding the practice of widow suicide *(sati)* after he witnessed the horrible death of his brother's wife. His study of Islam led him to conclude that idolatry was undesirable, and he moved toward a strict form of Hindu monotheism. This man of considerable intellect could read Persian, Arabic, Hebrew, and Greek, in addition to Sanskrit and Pali, and devoted serious study to Buddhism and Christianity as well.

After Roy died two important organizers succeeded him. Devendranath Tagore (1817–1905) joined the Samaj disillusioned with his study of both European philosophy and Vedanta, hoping for a reformed Hinduism. What he found was an organization still rife with practices he abhorred, including blatant devotionalism, idolatry, and caste exclusivism. He then steered a course toward reforming the reform organization, and the result would eventually be called the Sadharan Brahmo Samaj (Universal Society of God).

Tagore's protege, the mystically inclined Keshab Chandra Sen (1838–84), gradually introduced various Christian ideas learned from missionary friends, including the doctrine of the Trinity and the sacraments of Baptism and the Eucharist. He nearly converted to Christianity but balked at the requirement of professing the uniqueness of Jesus. Meanwhile he parted company with Tagore over the issue of social reform and began an offshoot of the Society that would repudiate Tagore's insistence on anti-Christian polemic.

Several reformers left, Vivekananda among them, the Brahmo Samaj, dissatisfied with its attempts to root out devotional and social abuses of traditional Hinduism. Other reformers had much in common with Gandhi, such as Shri Aurobindo Ghosh (1872–1950) of Bengal. After extensive study at Cambridge University, Shri Aurobindo returned to India and founded a famous ashram (a residential facility not unlike a monastery). His life's work was a reinterpretation of Hinduism in light of his study of European philosophy. In contrast to Shri Aurobindo's "modernism" is the more traditionalist reform of Ramana Maharshi (1879–1950), born Venkataramana Aiyar. This south Indian devotee of Shiva the Dance King sought to reinstate Upanishadic tradition as the heart of Hinduism. Many in both India and elsewhere still revere him as a saint.

92. What was Hinduism's role in the story of the independence and partitioning of India?

The state of Bengal is a good place to start, because of its importance as the birth place of several devotional and reform movements and the dramatic changes that occurred when it was divided as part of the partitioning of India. Along with the proliferation of reformist organizations came important developments in Hindu scholarship, as well as the growth and strengthening of various ancient sectarian religious groups. Much of the nascent Hindu nationalism was aimed against European culture and imperialism, but significant non-Hindu minorities, especially the Muslims, were growing uneasy with escalating Hindu aspirations. One result during the first half of this century was a new Muslim nationalism.

Elsewhere in India Hindu nationalism was growing as well, nowhere more noticeably than under the influence of Bal Gangadhar Tilak (1856–1920). During the early 1900s, Tilak mounted an often murderous campaign against British rule in the state of Maharashtra. For inspiration he looked to the Marathi hero Shivaji (1627–80), who had withstood the Mughal dynasty to form India's last authentically Hindu polity. Tilak's rhetoric worried his Muslim neighbors, because although he shared Gandhi's love of the *Bhagavad Gita,* he preferred an interpretation that emphasized an active role for the warrior caste. His militancy spawned the Hindu Mahasabha and its military wing, Rashtriya Svayamsevak Sangha, in the 1920s.

Tilak represented an extreme against which moderates like Gandhi and his ally Jawaharlal Nehru (1889–1964) would fight and ultimately prevail. They were, however, dealing with redoubtable representatives of a Muslim nationalism dating back to the initial inspiration of Sayyid Ahmad Khan (1817–98), promoted by poet Muhammad Iqbal (d. 1938), and forged into a modern political force by Muhammad Ali Jinnah (1876–1948), the Father of Pakistan. In 1947, British rule ended and a separate two-part Muslim state came into being, half of the state of Bengal carved off as East Pakistan and a large chunk of northwestern India as West Pakistan. Twenty-four years later East Pakistan declared itself an independent Bangladesh. For several tragic years after partition and independence, Muslim refugees from India and Hindu refugees from the new independent state suffered the horrors of relocation, displacement, and persecution.

93. The Beatles became interested in Hinduism through the Maharishi Mahesh Yogi. Was the Maharishi's teaching an authentic reflection of Hinduism? What about the followers of Bhagwan Shree Rajneesh and Meher Baba—are they Hindus?

Maharishi Mahesh Yogi (b. c. 1911) founded a movement best known as Transcendental Meditation (TM), also called the Spiritual Regeneration Movement. His teaching was based on the tradition of advaita Vedanta, according to which one pursues the "way of knowledge" through disciplined meditation. In TM, seekers receive a special mantra when they are initiated by the guru; the mantra forms the core of their meditative practice as they gradually shed their illusions about body and true self. The Maharishi (an honorific title meaning "great seer") traveled to England in 1958 and within ten years or so the Beatles had become his most famous followers. After several visits to the Maharishi's ashram in India for further instruction, the "Fab Four" began to incorporate Hindu themes into some of their lyrics. George

Harrison learned to play the sitar well enough to add it to some instrumental tracks, lending a distinctively Indian sound, and after going solo even wrote a couple of outright devotional songs, such as "My Sweet Lord," laced with Sanskrit God-talk.

The Beatles were not particularly interested in converting to Hinduism as such, but were looking, like so many of their generation, for spiritual connections in a disconnected world. After 1970, proponents of the Science of Creative Intelligence began preaching the psychological benefits of Transcendental Meditation. For many practitioners, TM's Hindu roots are largely irrelevant, and they focus on a kind of religiously nondescript meditation or centering technique, occasionally combined with less than persuasive claims that TM allows them to levitate.

The Rajneesh Foundation is the official name of the followers of Bhagwan Shree Rajneesh (1931–90) who started a center for meditation in Poona not far from Bombay. During the 1970s his method of "chaotic meditation" gained popularity in the United States. Meher Baba (1894–1969), also from Poona, became most famous for not uttering a word for the last forty-four years of his life, though he did give lectures by means of sign and gesture. He claimed to be the divine avatar of his time. Small groups of followers in the United States have maintained devotion to the Baba but do not necessarily follow recognizably Hindu teaching or ritual practice.

94. What is the story of the Hare Krishna movement?

Many Americans will recall seeing groups of saffron-robed, shaven-headed young men and women on college campuses or other public places playing small drums and tiny finger cymbals and chanting "Hari Krishna, Hari Rama…." Some will recall being approached in an airport by a young man or woman who wanted to speak about the good news of Krishna and exchange a copy of some religious text for a donation. Popularly dubbed the "Hare Krishnas," these were people on a mission. Though they are no longer nearly so visible, partly because of complaints about their zeal that resulted in city ordinances of various kinds, the American followers of Krishna are still active but evidently adding fewer new members than in the 1960s and 70s. The organization represents a contemporary manifestation of the ancient Hindu devotional tradition of bhakti.

Swami A. C. Bhaktivedanta (1896–1977) founded the International Society for Krishna Consciousness (ISKCON). His story is a fine example of a twentieth-century adaptation of the classic four stages of life. The former pharmaceutical salesman became a sannyasin in 1959, some thirty-seven years after being initiated by a Vaishnava guru spiritually descended from Chaitanya (1486–1533), one of Krishna's most celebrated devotees. In 1965, Bhaktivedanta came to the United States and began laying the foundations of ISKCON. Within a few years the organization had local chapters across the United States. Aspirants and devotees attached to the temples the guru founded were either students intent on pursuing a monastic life in community or householders who were married and lived independently.

In order to insure the continuing spread of the movement, Bhaktivedanta "ordained" a group of disciples as initiating gurus whose task was to perpetuate the lineage. He was thereby addressing a critical issue, that of spiritual legitimacy and links to Indian tradition. The Swami had sought to establish the movement in India during the 1970s with temples in two holy cities, Krishna's birthplace, Vrindavan, and Chaitanya's home in Mayapur, thus incorporating ISKCON institutionally within the orbit of mainstream devotion to Krishna. Still a missionary movement, ISKCON has toned down its proselytizing methods considerably.

95. I drive by a Vedanta Society building on my way to work. What is it and what happens there?

Swami Vivekananda founded the Vedanta Society in 1895 while visiting New York City. Under the leadership of the Ramakrishna Order and its Mission, the Vedanta Society teaches a type of neo-Hindu reinterpretation of Shankara that has developed a socially active role for a newly conceived style of sannyasin. No longer withdrawn from a world that is illusory in any case, the monks of the Order engage in serious social work. In addition the Vedanta Society serves its public by offering training in Advaita meditation, centerpiece of the traditional way of knowledge, and by providing lectures on related philosophical themes. Vivekananda had been much influenced by non-Indian philosophical writings and the Society's neo-Hindu teachings reflect that. Though Ramakrishna himself did not stress Vedanta and its methods, the Mission has focused on them rather than on the preferred method of their patron saint, the way of devotion. On the mantle of the meeting room of the Vedanta Society in St. Louis stands a picture of Ramakrishna, who has been raised, some claim, to divine stature. Most Vedanta Society facilities are under the direction of a resident Swami of the Ramakrishna Order. In some instances, the Swami also functions as spiritual guide for the monks in training who aspire to become full members of the Order.

96. Right down the road from my home is a newly and elaborately expanded Hindu temple. Is Hinduism growing rapidly in the United States? What do Hindus do in their temples?

Many American cities now have Hindu communities large and wealthy enough to fund impressive buildings for social and religious activities. The temple complexes I have visited have facilities for meetings and lectures, child care, social gatherings including meals that can be prepared in the kitchen, and small libraries and/or bookstores, all in addition to serving the specific ritual needs associated with a temple. American Hindus include both Shaiva and Vaishnava communities, sometimes worshipping in the same temple. Most members of these temple communities are immigrants and their children from India, with a few converts from other ethnic backgrounds. Converts to the International Society of Krishna Consciousness and the Vedanta Society, on the other hand, are largely of non-Indian background. Here we have a good example of the practical difference between these two avowedly missionary Hindu movements and the more typically nonproselytizing mode of the majority.

Ritual activities in the temples vary according to sectarian affiliation. In most cases, the chief mode of worship is *puja,* including devotional offerings, prayers of petition, and worshipful attentiveness to the deity enshrined there. A fine example is the Shri Venkateshvara temple in the Pittsburgh area. Begun in 1972 and dedicated seven years later, it is one of the most elaborate in the country. Its architectural style is characteristic of south Indian temples, with a monumental tower gateway called a *gopuram,* an elegant *shikhara* spire over the womb chamber and two smaller spires over chambers for secondary deities. Although the temple is mainly Vaishnava, dedicated to Vishnu as Lord of Venkata ("Hill Lord," one of many epithets), it includes Shaiva imagery. Just inside the main doorway and to the left stands Ganesha, guardian of comings and goings. In the auditorium beneath the temple proper, Shiva the Dance King presides over the place in which weddings and concerts are held. In the lower area are murals depicting the ten avatars and the goddesses Lakshmi, Sarasvati, and Parvati. Moving toward the main area of the temple once inside the gopuram, worshippers ascend one set of steps to a platform over which a protective image of Garuda, Vishnu's eagle-like mount, presides. Vishnu's four-armed image resides in the central womb chamber, with consorts Lakshmi in the form of Padmavathi (Lotus Dweller) in the chamber to the left and Andal, also known as Bhu the earth deity, to the right. Andal was a historical figure, the female Alvar poet-saint, in whom Bhu became incarnated. All the signs indicate that the patrons of this temple come largely, if not entirely, from south India. Estimates as to the Hindu population of the United States range between five hundred thousand and a million.

97. Are there any distinctively Hindu views on environmental issues?

Hindu tradition has from the most ancient times considered the earth, indeed all that Christians would call "creation," sacred, even so far as to regard it as the very body of God. But that tradition has not always had a clear and direct influence on public policy. A more specific example might help here. Mahatma Gandhi was a sort of Hindu environmentalist before the term came into common usage. His concern for simple living, labor intensive, small-scale industry, and the use of only as much as one needed to maintain health and strength all have important environmental implications. For Gandhi social concern was deeply rooted in his conviction of the sacredness of life. His use of nonviolent political means began with the doctrine of noninjury and was adapted as a principle of social ethics. Gandhi was part of an ancient heritage of teachings with potentially great impact on the environment. One can point to a number of traditional Hindu teachings that apply directly to respect for and care of the living world.

Translating those teachings into action is another matter. Start at the symbolic end of the spectrum, with the age-old practice of sprinkling the cremated ashes of millions of people a year into India's rivers and the undying belief that one can still bathe safely in the sacred waters. Then move toward the other extreme, where market forces rule. With its enormous and growing population—almost four times that of the United

States on less than half the real estate—India's natural resources and life-space are under enormous strain. A growing middle class now brings increased buying power to the marketplace in search of air conditioners and refrigerators. In a country already strapped for ways to maintain sustainable use of resources, whose power plants even now churn out clouds of dense black soot, those concerned with environmental policy face an unimaginable challenge. Hinduism's reservoir of wisdom about the unity of life is deep enough, but like the environmentally pertinent teachings of other traditions it is frequently overwhelmed by socioeconomic realities.

98. There has been increasing interest lately, among Christians at least, in the connections between spirituality and health. Does Hinduism have anything to say about that?

Advances in medical technology have made tremendous strides toward reducing the number of diseases long considered incurable. People who have access to the fruits of those developments are living longer, healthier lives, but the increasing depersonalization of some aspects of health care sometimes merely replaces one kind of suffering with another. Traditional spiritualities, whether Christian or Hindu, seek ways to help people understand that technical advances that merely postpone death are not necessarily advances at all. Hinduism claims a vast reservoir of wisdom that can be suitably adapted to the needs of contemporary "pastoral care" in the context of healing. For most Hindus, whether in rural India or in crowded cities where health care resources are stretched thin and technical advances are happening very slowly, traditional methods of healing mind and body remain very important.

Traditional Hindu healing tends to be homeopathic (fighting fire with fire), but does not altogether rule out allopathic treatments (fighting fire with water). Disease of any kind suggests an imbalance of energies symbolized by wind, fire, water, and earth. The earliest source for addressing many such imbalances is the *Ayurveda* ("life knowledge," a secondary text associated with the scripture called the *Atharva Veda*), with its formulae for the ritual use of hundreds of natural remedies. Like other traditional systems, Ayurvedic medicine rests on a metaphysical foundation that analyzes all things into various sets of features depending on which aspect of existence one is addressing: the five elements of the physical universe, the seven bodily substances of physiology, the three "sheaths" of human anatomy, or the three humors that make up temperament. Modern medicine has tended to dismiss such models as unscientific and has replaced them with others that are, unfortunately, impersonal, non-holistic, and artificial. Current interest in spirituality and health care is concerned to reintegrate the metaphysical with the physical.

Traditional Hindu healing presupposes that even when physical manifestations of disease are clear and undeniable, one has ultimately to address the spiritual causes of the imbalance. This is no simplistic recourse to magic, but a result of the conviction that all things are connected and that, beneath all the sense data that modern medicine collects, lies the prior reality of forces not so easily quantified. We are beginning to appreciate some of the larger ramifications of physical disease as we acknowledge their social aspects—what we prefer to call public health dimensions. Hinduism's traditional healing takes a further step in that direction, teaching that so long as one addresses only the symptoms no genuine healing occurs.

99. What languages do contemporary specialists in Hinduism need to study?

Languages from two very different linguistic families are especially important for scholars whose principal work is the study of Hinduism. First and foremost are a cluster of Indo-European languages including Vedic, Sanskrit, and several related vernacular languages called the Prakrits. Sanskrit's relationship to Vedic is analogous to that of Attic Greek to the language of the Homeric epics. Virtually everyone who studies mainly Hinduism begins with Sanskrit, which is to Hinduism what Arabic is to Islam—the language of divine revelation as well as the sacred tongue of ritual. Even the name of the alphabet in which Sanskrit is written, *devanagari,* meaning "city of the gods," signals its sacred character. Dating from around 300 B.C.E. according to some scholars, Sanskrit is closely related to the language of the Vedas, but is a synthetic language "constructed" or "elaborated" (a root meaning of *samskrita*) by a grammarian named Panini (c. 300 B.C.E.) into a formal system.

A language as ancient as Sanskrit naturally has a complex history, as even a much younger tongue like English has, and scholars often specialize in texts from one or other period such as the Epic or Classical. Its position

within Hindu religious life is like that of Latin in Christendom, in that San-
skrit remained the language of liturgy and teaching for centuries; unlike
Latin, Sanskrit may never have been a truly "living" vernacular language at
all, but merely an artificial scholastic argot of the priestly class. Finally,
Sanskrit has been important theologically in that important thinkers, like
Bhartrihari (c. 570–651), have constructed a theology called Word or
Sound-Monism on the basis of their analyses of the language. Alongside
Sanskrit developed the so-called Prakrits (from a root that means "natural"
or "organic"). While Sanskrit was the hieratic tongue of Hinduism, the
Prakrits became the language in which Buddhists and Jains wrote their
sacred texts. In Sanskrit theater, women and lower class characters spoke
Prakrit. The most important Prakrits for Hindu studies are the later regional
languages such as Hindi, Bengali, Gujarati, and Marathi.

In addition, a large family of non-Aryan languages known as Dravidian are especially important for scholars who specialize in the religious history and culture of southern India. Tamil is the most important
for both literary and colloquial purposes, followed by Telugu, Kannada,
and Malayalam. Indologists have nearly 900 distinct languages and
dialects to choose from as they contemplate the possibilities for
research. Anthropologists and historians use any of dozens of other
Prakrit and Dravidian nonliterary vernaculars for field work. Some
scholars of Hinduism work in more than one language, typically in com-
binations such as Sanskrit and Tamil (roughly the linguistic equivalent
of a Biblical scholar's use of both Hebrew and Greek, languages from
two completely different families). Choice of languages naturally
depends on the geographical area and historical period of a scholar's
research interest.

100. Is it possible, or advisable, for a Christian or other non-Hindu to simply pick and choose attractive aspects of Hinduism and try to integrate them into his or her confessional beliefs?

Though I am convinced of the importance of studying the world's
religious traditions, I am equally convinced that a smorgasbord
approach to personal spiritual fulfillment is not helpful for most people.
My reservations arise out of what some might call a "classicist" view of
religious systems, a view that discerns an underlying inner logic and
consistency in the beliefs around which faith communities grow. That is

not to suggest that one can draw tidy boundaries between religions as though they were so many canned goods on a grocery store shelf, indicating neatly where, say, Hinduism ends and Buddhism begins. There is no such thing as "pure" Christianity or Islam or Hinduism. Nor do I believe that the faith of any one person who identifies him or herself as a Hindu, for example, is quite the same as that of any other person who chooses the same identifier. Religious belief is infinitely more complex, and there is a sense in which we all fashion our unique ways of explaining the meaning of human existence out of bits and pieces we find along the way. We all "construct" our realities, draw our own maps; that's what being an individual is all about. In fact, it would not surprise me to hear a Christian and her Hindu friend report that they found that in their personal beliefs they were closer to each other than to some of the people who worshipped in the same temple or church.

There is, however, more to religious belief than the kind of personal choice that orders "one from column A, one from column B." Many individuals obviously choose to move away from their religious communities of origin and become converts to other communities. But such conversion nearly always involves the choice of one community support system to replace another or to supply the sense of community an individual may have found wanting in his or her previous religious affiliation. The point is that when most people draw deliberately on a new faith tradition, they buy the whole package. Even if they have minor reservations about certain elements, they are generally willing to make allowances or let themselves to be persuaded otherwise.

Secondly, religious symbols get their meaning from context, not merely from their aesthetic appeal or the kind of novelty that individual seekers often take for the expression of some truth never dreamt of in their religious communities of origin. Suppose I see a statue of Shiva the Dance King, hear its story, and tell myself I will appropriate it for my own collection of God-images since I prefer to think of the creator God as playing rather than as sweating over a lump of clay. Here we come back to the earlier question about whether all religious searching might simply come together in the melting pot of mysticism. It might be important in this instance for me to understand that the Dancing Shiva has underscored for me the notion of God's absolute freedom—a notion already very much part of my Catholic heritage—but that the God I meet when I die will not be this name and form called Shiva. It matters more than a little how one identifies oneself with respect to religious belief, if only because a person who chooses to believe religiously ultimately has to believe *something* coherent. A patchwork of images ordered *a la carte* doesn't quite fit the bill.

101. What have you, as a specialist in religious studies, learned from Hinduism that has made a personal impact on you?

Most of all my study of religious traditions like Hinduism, Buddhism and Islam has been a luxury, an enormous privilege, and a source of grace and wonderment. The longer I enjoy the luxury of being able to make a living dipping into these wellsprings of wisdom, the more I find myself reflecting on unexplored possibilities in my own Catholic tradition. Hinduism has presented a number of distinctive invitations to revisit my own reasons for and ways of believing. But first let me put this in context.

People who talk (as I have here) about Hinduism as though it were one large family of related belief systems often make assumptions about this larger "Hinduism" that no believing Hindu who belongs to one of its many sub-communities ever would. For most individual believers, Hinduism does not mean the whole amazing panoply of names and forms and ritual and history described in these pages; it means this festival celebrating this deed of this god or goddess who watches over this family in this town. So long as one bears in mind this gaping chasm between the experience of most Hindus and academic constructions of "Hinduism," one can come away from the study truly graced and enriched in many ways.

Given that, let me mention three of many aspects of this greater Hinduism that have been personally moving and enriching both intellectually and spiritually. First, I have been intrigued by the tradition's flexibility, though some might call its ability to subsume virtually every religious idea or manifestation in its path over the centuries rather a form of doctrinal imperialism. Some critics see the tradition as open to the charge of wholesale syncretism. On the other hand, Hinduism has also had its share of dogmatism despite the lack of an official central magisterium. The dominance of the Brahmanical priesthood has often bolstered an oppressive status quo. Still, taken as a whole, the greater Hinduism has over the centuries grown and incorporated much that is new while remaining somehow recognizably "Hindu."

Second, the larger Hindu tradition represents an extraordinarily rich gallery of imagery of the divine. Other traditions sometimes seem, by contrast, to focus on restricting the collective imagination to a select few images of the deity and on damage control when constraint fails. The Hindu theological imagination flows on virtually undammed by the kinds of cautionary signals that are the stuff of Christian and Islamic theology, for example. Here the centrality of narrative in Hindu theology spells the difference. Other traditions also possess rich heritages of story, but rarely in anything like the profusion that Hinduism embraces as sacred scripture. More than that, Hindu tradition has not only countenanced but positively encouraged visual arts to match the verbal. The result is a feast for the eyes and imagination.

Finally, as individuals, Hindus are not necessarily inclined to be more tolerant of human diversity than the rest of us. Hindus in India are just as capable of hating their Muslim or Christian fellow citizens as are the Catholics and Protestants of Northern Ireland, or the Israeli Jews and Palestinian Muslims. But the greater Hinduism represents for me a style of religious tolerance, at least as an ideal, in a way no other tradition does. Hinduism's history has been relatively free of large scale proselytizing. Naturally this matter is not as simple and clear as I am tempted to make it here, but I think the general point is valid.

I do not suggest that features like these are missing in other traditions, merely that the greater Hinduism manifests them to such a remarkable degree that they remain my overwhelming impression of this amazing tradition. All of these features, and many more, have continually challenged me to look with wider eyes at other traditions I study as well as at my own.

TIMELINE OF HINDU HISTORY

c. 2750 B.C.E.	Growth of civilization in the Indus Valley
c. 1500	Aryan Invasions
1200–900	Composition of the Vedic Samhitas
900–500	Composition of the later parts of the Samhitas, of the Brahmanas, and the Upanishads
c. 500	Aryans as far south as Sri Lanka
500–200	Epic poetry: *Mahabharata* (Bhagavad Gita), *Ramayana*
327–325	Alexander the Great invades India
322	Chandragupta founds Mauryan Empire
100–100 C.E.	Rise of Bhakti Literature
300–600	Composition of some of the Puranas in their present form
647	Fall of Gupta Empire
680	Flourishing of Tamil Bhakti Movement
788–820	Shankara, Theology of nonduality
800–900	Rise of Hindu Orthodoxy
1017–1138	Ramanuja, Theology of qualified nonduality
1175	First Muslim Empire in India
1486–1533	Chaitanya, Krishna-Bhakti
1498	Vasco da Gama visits India
1526	Rise of Mughal Dynasty
1653	Taj Mahal completed
1657	Dara Shikoh translates the Upanishads into Persian
1690	British found Calcutta
1707	Decline of Mughal power
1836–1886	Ramakrishna, "All religions can lead to God-realization"
1869–1948	Mahatma Gandhi
1885	Indian National Congress
1947	Indian Independence; Creation of Pakistan

SUGGESTIONS FOR FURTHER READING

Bagwe, Anjali. *Of Woman Caste: The Experience of Gender in Rural India*. London: Zed Books, 1995.

Blurton, T. Richard. *Hindu Art*. Cambridge, Mass.: Harvard University, 1993.

Clooney, Francis X , S.J. *Hindu Wisdom for All God's Children*. Mary-knoll, N.Y.: Orbis Books, 1998.

Desai, Prakash N. *Health and Medicine in the Hindu Tradition*. New York: Crossroad, 1989.

Doniger, Wendy. *Asceticism and Eroticism in the Mythology of Shiva*. London: Oxford University, 1973.

―――――. *The Rig Veda: An Anthology*. Harmondsworth: Penguin Books, 1981.

―――――, trans. *Hindu Myths: A Sourcebook*. New York: Crossroad, 1981.

Eck, Diana L. *Banaras, City of Light*. New York: Alfred A. Knopf, 1982.

―――――. *Darshan: Seeing the Divine Image in India,* 2d ed. Chambers-burg, Pa.: Anima Books, 1985.

―――――. *Encountering God: A Spiritual Journey from Bozeman to Benares*. Boston: Beacon, 1993.

Hawley, John Stratton and Donna Marie Wulff, eds. *Devi: Goddesses of India*. Berkeley: University of California, 1996.

―――――, ed. *Sati, the Blessing and the Curse*. New York: Oxford University, 1994.

Hopkins, Thomas J. *The Hindu Religious Tradition*. Belmont, Calif.: Wadsworth, 1971.

Kinsley, David. *Hindu Goddesses: Visions of the Divine Feminine in the Hindu Religious Tradition*. Berkeley: University of California, 1988.

―――――. *Hinduism: A Cultural Perspective*. Englewood Cliffs, N.J.:

Prentice Hall, 1982.

———. *The Sword and the Flute—Kali and Krsna: Dark Visions of the Terrible and the Sublime in Hindu Mythology*. Berkeley: University of California, 1975.

Kramrisch, Stella. *Manifestations of Shiva*. Philadelphia: Philadelphia Museum of Art, 1981.

Lipner, Julius. *Hindus: Their Religious Beliefs and Practices*. London: Routledge, 1994.

Michell, George. *The Hindu Temple: An Introduction to its Meaning and Form*. London: Paul Elek, 1977.

Mitter, Sara S. *Dharma's Daughters: Contemporary Indian Women and Hindu Culture*. New Brunswick, N.J.: Rutgers University, 1996.

Olivelle, Patrick, trans. *Upanishads*. Oxford: Oxford University Press, 1996.

Panikkar, Raimundo. *The Vedic Experience*. London: Darton, Longman and Todd, 1977.

Pereira, Jose. *Hindu Theology: A Reader*. Garden City, N.Y.: Image Books, 1976.

Pintchman, Tracy. *The Rise of the Goddess in the Hindu Tradition*. Albany: State University of New York Press, 1994.

Powell, Barbara. *Windows into the Infinite: A Guide to the Hindu Scriptures*. Fremont, Calif.: Asian Humanities Press, 1996.

Ramanujan, A. K., trans. *Speaking of Shiva*. Baltimore: Penguin Books, 1973.

Ranade, R. D. *Mysticism in India: The Poet Saints of Maharashtra*. Albany: State University of New York Press, 1996.

Zaehner, R. C. *The Bhagavad Gita*. London: Oxford University Press, 1973.

———. *The Hindu Scriptures*. New York: E. P. Dutton, 1966.

SELECT GLOSSARY OF HINDU SANSKRIT TECHNICAL TERMS

Anada: "bliss, delight"; a characteristic of ultimate reality and the liberated soul.

Artha: worldly success, wealth, influence; second of the four laudable goals of life.

Asana: a seated "posture" assumed as part of spiritual practice, as in yoga and sculpture.

Ashram(a): a place of spiritual retreat; term for the four "stages of life."

Atman: the "in-divisible" and indestructible spiritual center of each being, and the ultimate "Self" underlying all reality.

Avatar(a): "crossing-over-downward"; a deity's (especially Vishnu's) descent into the world of human experience.

Bhakti: "participation"; devotional relationship to one's chosen deity; a major "path" to liberation.

Brahman: Ultimate Reality enveloping all appearances of multiplicity.

Brahmin: member of the priestly class.

Chit: spiritual "consciousness"; a characteristic of ultimate reality and the liberated soul.

Darshan(a):   "seeing, being seen by" the deity; goal of devotional practice; philosophical school.

Dharma: concentration, meditation; one of the eight "limbs" of yogic practice.

Guna: "strand"; an attribute or quality according to one classic tripartite Hindu analysis of phenomenal reality into passion, goodness, darkness.

Guru: from root meaning "grave, heavy"; a spiritual guide or teacher.

Jati: "birth-status"; one of the distinguishing features in social stratification, often called "caste."

Jnana: "knowledge"; insight into the spiritual meaning of things; one of the principal "paths" to liberation.

Kama: "pleasure"; one of the four legitimate goals of life.

Karma: "action"; ritual or ethical conduct and the consequences thereof; one of the traditional "paths" to liberation.

Marga: path, way; method of spiritual progress toward liberation.

Moksha: liberation from the round of rebirth, ultimate goal of Hindu spiritual practice.

Namarupa: "name-form"; a reference to the appearances under which the deity condescends to be known, out of deference to human need.

Puja: ritual worship of one's chosen deity, either at home or in a temple or other shrine.

Sadhu: "accomplished one"; an individual who has achieved liberation in this life.

Samsara: "journeying"; the endless round of rebirth from which Hindus seek to be free.

Sannyasi: renunciant; the fourth of the traditional life-stages or *ashramas.*

Sat: "being," along with consciousness (*chit*) and bliss (*anada*), one of the characteristics of Ultimate Reality.

Shakti: "feminine energy"; generic name of female divine consorts.

Shruti: "heard"; referring to the authoritative status of the earliest categories of sacred scriptures, the Vedas and Upanishads.

Smriti: "remembered"; the later scriptures, including the epics and *puranas*, for example.

Varna: "color"; referring to one of the four major traditional socio-religious distinctions: priest, warrior, merchant, peasant; popularly but erroneously understood as "caste."

Vedanta: "end of the Veda"; originally referring to the Upanishads; a school of thought dedicated to the path of knowledge.

Yoga: "joining, harnessing"; system of physical and spiritual disciplines practiced by a *yogi.*

INDEX

(This index contains selected persons, places, events and themes to help you find your way through the text. Numbers following entries indicate the *question* in which that entry is found.)

abortion: 42
Adhvaryu (Vedic priests) : 3
Aditya(s): 5; *see also* Atharva
advaita: see Vedanta, *advaita*
Agni (terrestrial fire god): 5, 6, 78, 83
aguna (vice): 38; *see also* evil; intention; law
ahimsa: (noninjury): 40; and asceticism: 41; in Jainism: 65; Gandhi on: 88
Akbar (d.1605): 71
Alexander the Great (d. 323 B.C.E.): 18
allegory, in Aranyakas: 7; *see also* interpretation; metaphor
Alvars (mystic saints): 96; and suicide: 42; poetry of: 57
androgyny: 46; *see also* sexuality
Angkor Thom: 19; *see also* temple(s)
Angkor Wat: 19; *see also* temple(s)
Aranyakas (Forest Treatises): 7; on ritualism: 11; and *jnana-marga:* 45
archaeology: 1
architecture: 18; and spirituality: 44, 60; of American temples: 96; *see also* temple(s); womb-chamber
Ardhanarishvara (Half-woman Lord): 82; *see also* Shiva
Arjuna: 16, 39
art(s): *see* architecture; dance; illustration; image(s); music; painting; poetry; sculpture
artha (wealth): 25, 37

Gujarati; Hindi; Kannada; Malayalam; Marathi; metaphor(s); Sanskrit; sound; Tamil; Telugu; Vedic
Laos: 19
last things: *see* theology, eschatology
law(s): 13; and Dharma: 35; against caste system: 36; and sin: 37; and philosophy: 55; *see also shastra(s);* Manu
Laws of Manu: *see shastra(s),* Laws of Manu; Manu
liberation: *see moksha*
life-stages: *see* stations
lila (play): 33, 48, 79
linga: 20, 31, 46, 82; *see also* Shiva

Madhva (d. 1278): 12, 21, 45; *see also* dualistic theism; monasticism, orders of
Madras: 18
magic: 5, 13, *see also* astrology
Mahabharata: 13, 16; and ethics: 39, 42; and drama: 62; and time: 64; on women: 70, 81; *see also* Vaishnavite Hinduism; *Bhagavad Gita*
Maharishi Mahesh Yogi (b. c. 1911): 1, 93
mahayuga: see yuga(s)
Majapahit Kingdom: 19
Malayalam (language): 99
Malaysia: 19
Mamallapuran, temple of: 18; *see also* Pallavas
mandala and temple architecture: 60; *see also* text(s)
mantra(s): 53; *see also* ritual
Manu: 35; *see also shastra(s),* Laws of Manu
Marathi (language): 57, 99
margas (spiritual paths): 44, 45
marriage and caste: 4, 36; and Shiva: 15; and *samkaras:* 28, 29; interreligious: 71; practices: 85; and polygamy: 86; *see also* family; ritual(s)
Martin Luther King, Jr. (d. 1968): 40
Marut(s) (lesser gods): 6
math(s) (urban monasteries): 21; *see also* monasticism; temple(s)
Mathura: 20; *see also* geography, sacred
Maurya Dynasty: 18
maya (power of creating illusion of multiplicity): 12; and spirituality: 45, 46; *see also* Vedanta

Surya (celestial god): 5, 17
sutra(s) (aphorisms): 13; and philosophy: 55

Tagore, Devendranath (d. 1905): 91
tamas (moral darkness): 38; *see also* evil
Tamil Hindus: 17, 18, 75; Alvars: 57, 79; language of: 57, 75, 79, 99
Tanjore temple of: 18; *see also* Shiva
Tantrism: 39, 59, 89
Taoism: 11, 43
tapas (heat): 41
teacher(s): 35, 50; *see also gurus*
Telugu (language): 99
temple(s) and Islam: 19; and monks: 21, 94; and rituals: 28, 31, 63, 80;
    and worship: 33, 52, 61, 67; and pilgrimage: 34; and spirituality: 48,
    60, architecture of: 54, 60, patronized by a Muslim: 71; destruction of:
    74; in the USA: 96; *see also* Angkor Thom; Angkor Wat; architecture;
    Khajuraho; Kanchipuram; Mamallapuran; *math(s);* Prambanam; rit-
    ual; *shikhara;* Tanjore; *upachara*
Thailand: 19
theater: *see* drama
theology and Hindu scriptures: 3; development of: 5, 56; and *Shatapatha*
    Brahmana: 7; popular: 13, 17; expansiveness of: 22; of salvation: 25,
    69; of time: 26; eschatology: 27; *via negativa:* 46; and philosophy: 55;
    compared to Christianity: 69; of incarnation: 69; *see also moksha;*
    orthodoxy; revelation
Tilak, Bal Gangadhar (d. 1920): 72, 92
time: *see* history, sacred
tirtha (crossing point): 34, 48; *tirthankaras:* 65
Tiruvalluvar (c. 300–400): 57
tradition and *smriti:* 13
transcendence in Hindu art: 58
Transcendental Meditation: 93; *see also* meditation; ritual(s)
tri-murti (triple form): 13, 14, 69; *see also* metaphor(s); *namarupa*
Tukarama (1607–49) hymns of: 57
tyaga (ignoring): 41; *see also* station(s) of life, renunciant

Udgatri (Vedic priest): 3
Ujjain: 20; *see also* geography, sacred; Shiva